T0370400

The Contract of Mutual Indifference

The Contract of Mutual Indifference

Political Philosophy after the Holocaust

NORMAN GERAS

VERSO
London • New York

First published by Verso 1998
© Norman Geras 1998
Paperback edition first published by Verso 1999
© Norman Geras 1999
All rights reserved

Verso
UK: 6 Meard Street, London W1V 3HR
USA: 180 Varick Street, New York NY 10014-4606

Verso is the imprint of New Left Books

ISBN 978-1-8598-4229-4

British Library Cataloguing in Publication Data
A catalogue record for this book is available from the British Library

Library of Congress Cataloging-in-Publication Data
A catalog record for this book is available from the Library of Congress

Typeset by SetSystems Ltd, Saffron Walden, Essex
Printed by Biddles Ltd, Guildford and King's Lynn

For Ben Marks

She suggested that she write a testimony ... so that the world would know about this horror that was taking place parallel to the peaceful existence of those who did not want to know, who could afford the illusion of a normal life, and of those who could deny that they were on a raft adrift in a sea of sorrow, ignoring, despite all evidence, that only blocks away from their happy world there were others, these others who live or die on the dark side.

Isabel Allende, *The House of the Spirits*

Contents

Contents

Foreword

The work here offered to the reader has been on my mind for some years, the circumstances in which its central idea first came to me being described on its first page. It stands, or falls, on its own. The argument it puts forward is a unitary one and pretty much self-contained. I have thought it appropriate, nevertheless, to include with it also three shorter pieces originally written for other purposes or occasions, for these treat of themes only touched on in passing in the essay which here precedes them, and I believe that they may usefully round out the general standpoint from which that essay has been written.

My intellectual debts on this occasion are principally two. My daughter Jenny Geras, alone, has shared with me from its inception the central idea I present in the following pages, and she has been talking to me about it on a regular basis ever since, as well as reading successive versions of the typescript. Eve Garrard, whom I met only when this work was already under way, has been most generous in her moral and intellectual support of my efforts to complete it and untiring in her discussion and questioning of – and sometimes indeed agreement with – aspects of my thinking. She too repeatedly read and commented on the draft of the work as it progressed. To have had two such loyal and stimulating interlocutors has been a matter of great good fortune for me.

I should also like to thank my students on the course which I have been teaching on the Holocaust for the last four years, and to say to any of them who happen to read this that it has been the pedagogic experience of my life, teaching that course, and this has been due in large part to the serious-mindedness and the moral maturity those taking the course have invariably brought to the consideration of difficult issues.

Sophie Geras, my daughter, as ever helps to balance my view of things with her unique and easy-going humour. And Adèle Geras's encouragement and support, her cheerful good temper and lifelong understanding, have been for their part incomparable.

My sincere gratitude to all concerned, with the customary authorial disclaimer.

Manchester, July 1997

1

The Contract of Mutual Indifference

The idea which I shall present here came to me more or less out of the blue. I was on a train some five years ago, on my way to spend a day at Headingley, and I was reading a book about the death camp Sobibor. Headingley, for those who may not know this, is a cricket ground in Leeds. At Sobibor between May 1942 and October 1943, the Germans killed a quarter of a million people. The particular, not very appropriate, conjunction involved for me in this train journey, reading about a place of death while bound one summer morning for an arena of entertainment, had the effect of fixing my thoughts on one of the more dreadful features of human coexistence, when in the shape of a simple five-word phrase the idea occurred to me.

It was not a welcome idea when it did. I have been unable to evade it since that day. Unwelcome as it is, I now give formal shape to it, and for the following familiar sort of reason: to face up to things unpleasant in the hope of finding an answer to them if there is one; of seeking, or prompting, some opposed or mitigating line of persuasion.

The idea I put forward, then, is not in its immediate content a happy one. Perhaps, further along, something positive also may be derived from it. If so, one may think of

the argument initially to be made here as being like a
segment, though a centrally important segment, of a larger
picture. The argument itself carries a preamble.

I 'Consider that this has been'

Early in Claude Lanzmann's movie *Shoah*, he and his interpreter speak to a man, Czeslaw Borowi, who has lived all his
life at Treblinka. Treblinka was the site of one of the three
death camps – Sobibor and Belzec were the other two – set
up for the so-called Aktion Reinhard, in which most of the
Jews of Warsaw, along with hundreds of thousands of the rest
of Polish Jewry, were murdered. Lanzmann asks Borowi
whether he and others working nearby, seeing the transports
of Jews arriving at the camp, were afraid (as he has indicated
they were for themselves) also for the Jews. The interpreter
gives Borowi's reply: 'Well, he says, it's this way: if I cut my
finger, it doesn't hurt him.'[1] Writing of this same period, the
period of the first great deportation from the Warsaw ghetto
in the summer of 1942, Adina Szwajger, a woman who
worked in the children's hospital there, recalls a scene: 'They
kept going past and it was a sweltering day ... On the
balcony of a house on Zelazna Street – there, on the other
side [of the ghetto wall] – a woman in a flowered housecoat
was watering plants in window boxes. She must have seen the
procession below, but she carried on watering her flowers.'[2]

This was July 1942. The next spring, in April 1943, the
Warsaw ghetto uprising began. The Germans set fire to the
ghetto, the remnant of its already doomed population trap-
ped within. Szwajger remembers that on a square nearby the
ghetto wall there was a merry-go-round. 'There were children sitting on this merry-go-round, while it went round and

1. Claude Lanzmann, *Shoah: An Oral History of the Holocaust*, New York 1985,
p. 25.
2. Adina Blady Szwajger, *I Remember Nothing More*, New York 1990, pp. 48–9.

4 THE CONTRACT OF MUTUAL INDIFFERENCE

round, and I could hear the music playing. Maybe I imagined it? The children were laughing and the people going by were smiling. And on the other side of the walls you could hear shooting.'[3] One Aaron Landau put on record at the time:

> I, who write these words
> I state, as an eye-witness
> that all the theatres, movie theatres,
> show-places, and all sorts of casinos
> and other places of amusement
> were open and operating according
> to their daily routines, at the
> time when up above, in the Warsaw skies,
> were rising coils of smoke from the
> burning ghetto, and inside burning alive
> tens of thousands of souls.[4]

Polish stories, but their theme is a continental one. Across the face of Europe, the victims and prisoners of the Third Reich feel abandoned. Testimony and memoir are thick with the sense of it. Most Germans will no longer associate with their Jewish friends, even under cover of darkness. Neighbours in a small Hungarian town observe the rules on not greeting or speaking to Jews; their doors are shut, the shades drawn on every window, when the Jews are taken away. In other places in Hungary also, people line the streets to watch them go. Many smile; some hide their smiles. Some throw stones, yell insults, spit. Some stand there crying, while others, afraid to stand and cry, go back into their houses.[5]

3. Ibid., p. 87.
4. Cited in Gay Block and Malka Drucker, *Rescuers: Portraits of Moral Courage in the Holocaust*, New York 1992, p. 160.
5. See, in turn, Frances Henry, *Victims and Neighbours*, South Hadley (Mass.) 1984, p. 24; Livia E. Bitton Jackson, *Elli: Coming of Age in the Holocaust*, London 1984, pp. 29, 32; Isabella Leitner, *Fragments of Isabella*, New York 1978, p. 13; Deborah Dwork, *Children With A Star*, New Haven 1991, p. 161.

And all over Germany, prisoners are marched back and forward: from the station to the concentration camp, from the camp to a work site, back to the camp, to the station for another camp. They see the outside world, see people. These people raise their fists against them. Or they spit, look the other way, turn their backs. Or *they* somehow do not 'see' – daily, a mass of wretched prisoners. Or they do see, but look on with indifference.[6] One day on a station platform at Weimar, Austrian Jews in transit between Dachau and Buchenwald are struck and kicked by the SS unit receiving them into its charge. Passengers on a train standing opposite crowd to the windows and applaud the SS. At a factory near the village of Troeglitz in the same region, young women, secretaries and typists there, point and laugh at a group of exhausted prisoners as they are about to be marched back to the camp. The women make abusive and sexually suggestive gestures at them.[7]

From the other side of the line now, we have the memory of someone, a child at the time, concerning the last twelve, mostly elderly, Jews in her town, assembling one morning on the instructions of the SS to be taken away. She recollects having called her parents to the window to see the departure of the couple who lived opposite. 'Her mother burst into tears and refused to come to the window while her father hastily pulled down the window shade.'[8] A woman, Erika S., who lived at Melk in Austria near the site of one of the sub-camps of Mauthausen, gives a frank account of the way she dealt with this physical proximity. She did sometimes see things, unavoidably. She tells of having felt pity in particular

6. Eugene Heimler, *Night of the Mist*, London 1961, p. 121; Micheline Maurel, *Ravensbrück*, London 1958, p. 88; Leitner, *Fragments of Isabella*, pp. 52–3; Hanna Lévy-Hass, *Inside Belsen*, Brighton 1982, pp. 19–20.
7. Leni Yahil, 'Jews in Concentration Camps in Germany Prior to World War II', in Y. Gutman and A. Saf, eds., *The Nazi Concentration Camps*, Jerusalem 1984, p. 87; Heimler, *Night of the Mist*, p. 86.
8. Henry, *Victims and Neighbours*, pp. 119–20.

for the plight of one Jew she observed, though a pity, it has to be said, that was mixed with something darker, namely amusement at the incongruous gait – 'like a circus horse' – forced upon this man by the pain in his bare feet and the whipping of the guards. Her general attitude, however, Erika S. characterizes as follows: 'I am happy when I hear nothing and see nothing of it. As far as I am concerned, they aren't interned. That's it. Over. It does not interest me at all.'[9]

Perhaps it is this attitude, this mental turning away, or perhaps the combination of all these responses to calamity brought upon others, that one of Saul Bellow's characters, Artur Sammler, a survivor of the shooting pits in Poland, has in mind when he says: 'I know now that humankind marks certain people for death. Against them there shuts a door.'[10]

In any event, just as in memoir and testimony, so also in a wider literature, in the novels, stories and poetry to which the Shoah has given rise, the bystander is a prominent figure – passive and indifferent, or worse. In Louis Begley's *Wartime Lies*, many of the inhabitants of Warsaw go up on their roofs to watch the 'entertainment' when the Germans bombard and burn the ghetto. And this is the scene as a German throws the narrator of Jiri Weil's *Life with a Star* off a tram in Prague: 'I looked around the tram. It was quite full. People's faces were set; they were looking at the floor, as if they were searching for a coin that had rolled under the wooden slats. Nobody spoke. Only his sharp voice was heard: "Get out, you swine..."' Ida Fink, in one of her most powerful stories, places the blank external perspective of an onlooker who has overheard a man's remark which he considers to be foolish and inconsequential in counterpoint with the internal world of this man and his wife and child as

9. Gordon J. Horwitz, *In the Shadow of Death: Living Outside the Gates of Mauthausen*, London 1991, pp. 112–14.
10. Saul Bellow, *Mr. Sammler's Planet*, London 1972, p. 230.

they are led away to be slain, and as, attempting to save the child's life at the last moment, the parents see her shot.[11]

There is also a memorable poem by Czeslaw Milosz on this subject, entitled 'Campo dei Fiori'.[12] The Campo dei Fiori in Rome is where Giordano Bruno was burned by the Inquisition in 1600. The poet remembers it one April day in Warsaw, on that same square with a carousel that we have already come across:

> ... that day I thought only
> of the loneliness of the dying,
> of how, when Giordano
> climbed to his burning
> he could not find
> in any human tongue
> words for mankind,
> mankind who live on.
>
> Already they were back at their wine
> or peddled their white starfish,
> baskets of olives and lemons
> they had shouldered to the fair,
> and he already distanced
> as if centuries had passed
> while they paused just a moment
> for his flying in the fire.
>
> Those dying here, the lonely
> forgotten by the world,
> our tongue becomes for them
> the language of an ancient planet.

---

11. Louis Begley, *Wartime Lies*, London 1992, pp. 102–4 (and cf. in this connection Block and Drucker, *Rescuers*, p. 159, and Martin Gilbert, *The Holocaust: The Jewish Tragedy*, London 1987, p. 661); Jiri Weil, *Life with a Star*, London 1990, p. 101; Ida Fink, 'A Spring Morning', in her *A Scrap of Time*, London 1988, pp. 39–47.
12. In Hilda Schiff, ed., *Holocaust Poetry*, London 1995, pp. 167–8; also in Szwajger, pp. 98–100.

> Until, when all is legend
> and many years have passed,
> on a new Campo dei Fiori
> Rage will kindle at a poet's word.

Consternation at the loneliness of the doomed, their own sense also of having been abandoned, these merge sometimes into a broader metaphysical theme. It is of the place of human suffering in an unnoticing cosmos. That the suffering should simply pass thus leaving the natural universe unaffected, although a fact which is itself entirely natural, is nevertheless a source of dismay or at any rate surprise; there is a feeling that it ought not to be so. A poem by W. H. Auden, 'Musée des Beaux Arts', relies by implication on the existence of such a sentiment. Auden writes there of the perceptive treatment of human suffering in the Old Masters: 'how it takes place/While someone else is eating or opening a window or just walking dully along'; how during even a dreadful martyrdom 'the torturer's horse/Scratches its innocent behind on a tree'; how, in Brueghel's *Icarus*, 'the sun shone/As it had to on the white legs disappearing into the green/Water'.[13]

In the annals of earlier Jewish sufferings, the protest at how things can be so is registered more than once. Following a massacre of over a thousand Jews in Mainz in 1096 – 'babes and sucklings who had not sinned or transgressed, the souls of innocent poor people' – Solomon bar Simson, in a lament that has been borrowed from by the historian Arno Mayer, wrote: 'Why did the heavens not darken and the stars not withhold their radiance, why did not the sun and moon turn dark?'[14] After the Kishinev pogrom of 1903, the poet Chaim Nachman Bialik observed in his turn: 'the sun is shining, the acacia is blooming and the slaughterer is slaughtering'.

13. W. H. Auden, *Collected Shorter Poems 1927–1957*, London 1969, pp. 123–4.
14. Arno Mayer, *Why Did the Heavens Not Darken?*, London 1990, pp. 26–7.

These words of Bialik's are then recalled in July 1942 in the diary of Abraham Lewin: on a 'lovely morning, the sky ... wonderfully beautiful' and, outside in the Warsaw ghetto during the first great deportation already aforementioned, 'shouts and screams'.[15] Simon Srebnik, one of only two or three survivors of the death camp at Chelmno where more than three hundred thousand Jews met their deaths, returns there many years later to bear witness. He comes to the place where, as he explains to Claude Lanzmann, 'they burned people', burned them in 'two huge ovens'. The setting is a rural one, deep green and bright summer, as he speaks: 'It was always this peaceful here. Always. When they burned two thousand people – Jews – every day, it was just as peaceful. No one shouted. Everyone went about his work. It was silent. Peaceful.'[16]

How to come to terms with the likes of it? 'So many children died of hunger, so many were gassed ... so many, so many ... Six million people died, and the sun didn't cease to shine!'[17]

Language of this kind is rather less common today, in the secular public discourses of the late twentieth century. For great numbers of its inhabitants the world is godless – either really or to all intents and purposes. If one does not believe in a sympathetic higher intelligence such as would protest its anguish through the very elements, if one does not, in some version of the pathetic fallacy, ascribe moral sentiments to nature itself, there is no reason at all why the sun should cease to shine on mass murder, on genocide, on anything. Even so, the expressions of a sentiment of incomprehension that it does not may have their point. Perhaps nature also stands in in this sort of observation and lament for the

15. Abraham Lewin, *A Cup of Tears: A Diary of the Warsaw Ghetto*, Oxford 1988, p. 138.
16. Lanzmann, *Shoah*, p. 6.
17. Szwajger, *I Remember Nothing More*, p. 136 (ellipses in the original).

inaction of people. Its lack of a sympathetic response may be offered, consciously or otherwise, as a metaphor for the failures of human beings, the indifference of the natural world as an image for the indifference of what we also sometimes refer to as 'the world' – of humanity. With *this* world, we like to think we are in another domain: not just brute thinghood, unresponsive natural causalities incapable of thought or feeling, but a sphere of intentionality and will, of the possibility of compassion, of indignation at avoidable suffering and injustice. Human beings, at least, need *not* remain peaceful, silent, in the presence of atrocity. Precisely in a godless world, it is they alone who can constitute a realm of saving norms and sustain these by their actions.

Indeed, on one conception of things, it is true even in a world in which God survives, that only by way of human action, human choices, can any benign purpose or normative realm be secured; it is the responsibility of our kind. Such is the view, for example, of Hans Jonas, reflecting on the implications of the Shoah for Jewish theological belief. The Divine, according to Jonas, in a kind of act of divestment or 'self-forfeiture' whose reasons we cannot know, has chosen to give itself over 'to the chance and risk and endless variety of becoming'. This has led by way of a long evolution, one 'carried by its own momentum', to 'the advent of man'; therewith, to 'the advent of knowledge and freedom' and 'to the charge of responsibility under the disjunction of good and evil'. The image of God here 'passes ... into man's precarious trust, to be completed, saved, or spoiled by what he will do to himself and the world'. Suffering and caring, Jonas contends, God should not any longer be thought of as being omnipotent.[18]

18. Hans Jonas, 'The Concept of God After Auschwitz: A Jewish Voice', in Alan Rosenberg and Gerald E. Myers, eds., *Echoes from the Holocaust: Philosophical Reflections on a Dark Time*, Philadelphia 1988, pp. 295–9. The essay is reprinted from *Journal of Religion* 67 (1987), pp. 1–13.

For humankind, in any case, it is freedom, and under the disjunction of good and evil. Jonas himself speaks in this context only in general terms. He does not deal specifically with the issue of those who look on at the wrongs and crimes of others, or who look away or do not 'see'. Two other writers, however, also calling on traditions of Jewish worship and belief, have for their part given this issue a quite special place and importance. They are Elie Wiesel and Primo Levi. I now want to present something of Wiesel's moral theology by outlining the story he tells in his book *The Town Beyond the Wall.* I shall then go on to consider some exhortatory lines by Primo Levi.

The central character of *The Town Beyond the Wall* is Michael, like Elie Wiesel himself a survivor of the Holocaust. He has returned secretly to his home town in Hungary during the Communist period. Each chapter of the book is styled a 'Prayer', a usage that is of double significance. As well as the straightforward meaning, it registers that the story of Michael's return is unfolding in his head (in memory, imagination and internal dialogue) while he is being subjected to a torture known as 'The Prayer'. This consists of keeping someone on their feet until their resistance is broken and is said to be known as it is 'because the Jews pray standing'.[19] Michael's arrest and incarceration have followed on an event only to be retailed to us late in the book, an event that is its pivotal, its resolving moment.

In the 'First Prayer', Michael remembers the town of his birth and childhood. On Friday night no one goes hungry there. 'Whoever is alone, whoever is a stranger, is invited by the people of the city to come and break bread with them.' Beggars, the poor and the dispossessed are 'the angels of peace of the Sabbath'. On one occasion, the boy is admonished by his father: 'Who does not live for man – for the man

19. Elie Wiesel, *The Town Beyond the Wall*, New York 1982, p. 7.

of today, for him who walks beside you and whom you can
see, touch, love and hate – creates for himself a false image
of God.'[20] At the same time as remembering, Michael vows
that he will not break under the torture, that he 'will not
betray'. He will not betray the friend, Pedro, who has made
possible his return and come back into Hungary with him,
and who he hopes may be still at large. 'That's always the
way it is', he thinks; 'when one man dies on his feet, another
is saved. Sometimes it's a friend, sometimes an unknown,
born tomorrow'.[21]

In keeping with a standpoint more general to Wiesel's
outlook, Michael is shown as being in dialogue with his God.
He has his prayers and also his quarrels with Him.[22] The
survivor of Auschwitz wants to blaspheme: 'I go up against
Him, I shake my fist, I froth with rage, but it's still a way of
telling Him that He's there, that He exists ... that denial
itself is an offering to His grandeur. The shout becomes a
prayer in spite of me.'[23] It is not the only one; there is a
quieter prayer as well. In the prehistory of the tale of the
return itself, we learn how strongly Michael wants to go back
to his birthplace. He would give ten years of his life to be
there for a single day. This is to see 'if it's still what it was',
but more than that, it is because he believes there is a truth
he will find there. The return having been arranged and on
the very point now of crossing the Hungarian border under
cover of night, Michael gives forth that other, silent prayer:
'God of my childhood, show me the way that leads to
myself'.[24]

The crossing successfully made, he goes about the town.

20. Ibid., pp. 13, 43.
21. Ibid., pp. 9, 21, 39.
22. See, in this connection, Elie Wiesel, 'Talking and Writing and Keeping
Silent', in John K. Roth and Michael Berenbaum, eds., *Holocaust: Religious and
Philosophical Implications*, New York 1989, p. 369.
23. *The Town Beyond the Wall*, pp. 114–15.
24. Ibid., pp. 119–20, 127.

He recognizes buildings, knows the colour of the sky; he returns to what was once the family home. The house is there but it is not any more the haven he remembers, and he no longer recognizes people in the streets. 'A stranger in my own city.' So why, after all, did he come back? Curiosity was part of it but this has been satisfied and Michael is sure he has not yet accomplished 'the essential task'. The main reason is 'somehow linked to a precise purpose, to a clear aim'. He is looking for something or someone without knowing what or whom.[25]

Then it comes to him. We are in the middle of 'The Last Prayer'. At the site of the old synagogue, Michael is remembering the Saturday when the Jews of the town were assembled here, 'last stop before boarding the death train'. Recalling this day, he is suddenly assailed by a memory and he knows at once, knows at last, that he has found what he was after. The memory is this: 'The window, the curtains, the face: in the house across the way. A spring day, sunny, the day of punishment, day of divorce between good and evil. Here, men and women yoked by misery; there, the face that watched them.' It is 'the *real* reason' for Michael's return.[26]

The face is representative. In its features Michael sees 'those who watched us depart for the unknown; those who observed us, without emotion, while we became objects ... and carefully numbered victims ... those who were permanently and merely spectators'. It is, however, an actual face as well. It is the face of a man who lived opposite the synagogue (and whose wife, we learn, was not watching at the window but, like that other woman remembered by her daughter, crying). For days the Jews coming and going, police beating women and children, children 'sick with thirst'; and this face at the window, 'cold, impersonal ...

25. Ibid., pp. 138–9, 141, 144.
26. Ibid., p. 148.

indifferent to the spectacle'. A question: 'How can anyone continue to embrace the woman he loves, to pray to God with fervour if not faith, to dream of a better tomorrow – after having seen *that?* After having glimpsed the precise line dividing life from death and good from evil?'[27]

In the sequel Michael confronts the man whose face at the window it was. He has found him still living in the same house. He delivers to him the message of contempt he carries from the dead. The man's duty, Michael says, was to choose: 'To fight us or to help.' As a mere spectator, he 'has nothing of the human in him: he is a stone in the street, the cadaver of an animal, a pile of dead wood'.[28]

The moral scope of this notion of 'the human' is then affirmed in the closing sequence of the book. In his cell in the jail to which this confrontation has led him but the torture now over, Michael is in despair. He is on the edge of madness. He resumes the conversation with the image of his friend Pedro that has recurred throughout the story. Pedro is already established in the reader's mind by this point as a character of great strength and importance for Michael. He is someone who speaks for an ethic of helping others: 'Many others. Obviously it isn't the number that matters. But then again, how can you help one man and not another? ... In rejecting, a man rejects himself; he isolates us all, and himself too.'[29] Pedro advises Michael to save himself by saving someone else, a fellow inmate who has lost his own reason and fallen silent: 're-create the universe. Restore that boy's sanity. Cure him. He'll save you.' Attempting a dialogue with the silent youth and finally getting some response, Michael ends by sharing the following thought with him: that the 'essence of man is to be a question', perhaps a question without an answer, and 'if two questions stand face to face,

27. Ibid., pp. 148–51, 156.
28. Ibid., pp. 153–64.
29. Ibid., p. 123 (and cf. pp. 118, 124).

that's at least something ... a victory'. He shares with this other also 'the necessity of clinging to humanity, never deserting humanity'. *The Town Beyond the Wall* closes with night receding and Michael having found the way he sought. For the other, we are told, 'bore the Biblical name of Eliezer, which means *God has granted my prayer.*'[30]

The human being is then, here, a question, in dialogue, now angry and now entreating, with God, in conversation with other human beings – human beings who in their generality are triumphant face to face as questions, fully themselves only when not rejecting the others of their kind. A crucial question for them, indeed, one challenging their humanity, is the question addressed to the spectator at the scene of evil. How continue life as normal after having seen *that?* How, if you are not a stone or pile of dead wood or a cadaver? How, in other terms, without disappearing into the insentient natural cosmos? The victim and survivor of the Holocaust thus puts his question, embodied in the literary form, so to say, of a prayer. To be indifferent is to stand condemned.

It is significant that another famous messenger from this same dark landscape saw fit to embody the identical moral issue and a similarly stern message into the form of a kind of prayer. I speak now of Primo Levi, and the form in his case is the poem rather than the novel: the poem 'Shemà'. It should be pointed out that Primo Levi's outlook, by contrast with that of Elie Wiesel, was resolutely secular. As he once explained succinctly to an interviewer: 'There is Auschwitz, and so there cannot be God.'[31] Levi nevertheless chose to take the words daily pronounced by religious Jews in both morning and evening prayer, words stating their most fun-

30. Ibid., pp. 172, 176–8.
31. Ferdinando Camon, *Conversations with Primo Levi*, Marlboro (Vermont) 1989, p. 68.

damental beliefs and duties, and to make fresh use of them in sombre admonition.

In the 'Shemà' itself – that is, the prayer[32] – believers affirm their belief in the one God and in His unity, and they are enjoined to take the words commanded to them upon their hearts. They are enjoined to repeat them to their children, and going to bed and rising, and when at home and in the street; and to write them on their doorposts and at their gates. Benefaction and disaster are foretold, respectively, for those who listen and those who stray. Adapting the prayer to his purpose, Levi refers us to the humanity of the Nazis' victims. Whether he does this simply by way of a humanist-type substitution, shifting from the idea of God to the figure of man and of woman, or whether he does it rather calling on a long Jewish tradition that sees entailed in the unity of God the unity also of humankind, it does not really matter. Either way, Levi issues an appeal to all those who live well-fed, warm and secure. He directs their attention to the stark image of the prisoner of the German *Lager*: to the image of a man labouring in the mud, dying 'at a yes or a no'; to the image of a woman 'without hair or name'. And he declares:[33]

> Consider that this has been:
> I commend these words to you.
> Engrave them on your hearts
> When you are in your house, when you walk on your way,
> When you go to bed, when you rise.
> Repeat them to your children.
> Or may your house crumble,
> Disease render you powerless,
> Your offspring avert their faces from you.

32. I am grateful to Harry Lesser for discussing the 'Shemà' with me, and for lending me the tape of a radio broadcast he has made on the subject.
33. Primo Levi, *Collected Poems*, London 1988, p. 9. Recent editions of Levi's *If This is a Man* also carry this poem, in a different translation.

Where Wiesel employs his character's dialogue with God in posing the question of the bystander, Primo Levi must be taken, in view of what we know about his outlook, to be making use only of the form of such dialogue, the form of the Jew speaking to his or her God. It remains true, all the same, that Levi looks to the most central and important prayer in Jewish tradition and, borrowing the force of its repeated call to keep what it commands close and ever present in the daily living of one's life, he attempts to deliver the most solemn pronouncement he can utter. It is an injunction to live with the terrible image of human violation before you, near you, on your heart. The very solemnity of the pronouncement and the malediction with which it concludes suggest that more is entrusted to these lines than only a wish to have the victims of the past held fast in memory, essential as that may be. Entrusted to them also is a live question and concern.

I shall come back immediately to the sort of accents in which we have now heard this question and concern articulated. They can still be heard today if you listen. I want to complete, first, the preliminary review that I have undertaken here, by indicating briefly how the preoccupation we have found in the literature of testimony and memoir, in the novels, the poetry and some of the theological reflection coming out of the Shoah, is prominent too in historical and sociological writing on the subject.

Part of the thesis, for example, of one eminent historian of the Third Reich, namely Ian Kershaw, is 'the indifference of the German people towards the fate of the Jews'. It was that indifference, according to him, nourished by a 'latent anti-semitism', which 'provided the climate within which spiralling Nazi aggression towards the Jews could take place unchallenged'.[34] This is not to say that the escalation toward

34. Ian Kershaw, *Popular Opinion and Political Dissent in the Third Reich*, Oxford 1983, pp. 274, 277.

18 THE CONTRACT OF MUTUAL INDIFFERENCE

genocide should be ascribed simply to the criminality of Hitler and other leading Nazis. It 'would not have been possible without the apathy ... which was the common response to the propaganda of hate'. Kershaw's point, however, is that 'dynamic hatred of the masses was unnecessary' to the process; their apathy 'sufficed to allow the increasingly criminal "dynamic" hatred of the Nazi regime the autonomy it needed to set in motion the holocaust'.[35] Most Germans, Kershaw says, 'probably thought little and asked less about what was happening to the Jews in the east'. As he has summed it up in a much-quoted formula, 'The road to Auschwitz was built by hate, but paved with indifference.'[36]

The same thesis is central to Zygmunt Bauman's book, *Modernity and the Holocaust.* Bauman expresses it as follows: 'Mass destruction was accompanied not by the uproar of emotions, but [by] the dead silence of unconcern.'[37] In his case, this is part of a more general view about the condition of modernity. The process of destruction worked, Bauman tells us, by 'increas[ing] the physical and mental distance between the purported victims and the rest of the population'. 'Evidently, moral inhibitions do not act at a distance', he says; and it is precisely the tendency of 'present-day industrial society to extend inter-human distance to a point where moral responsibility and moral inhibitions become inaudible'.[38]

Bauman has developed this viewpoint in a penetrating and widely admired book, but he is not the first or the only sponsor of it. Other analysts of the social aetiology of the Holocaust have argued similarly. Thus, referring to 'a society where everyone is a stranger to everyone else', George M. Kren has written: 'The indifference that much of the popu-

35. Ibid., pp. 371–2.
36. Ibid., pp. 364, 277.
37. Zygmunt Bauman, *Modernity and the Holocaust*, Cambridge 1991, p. 74.
38. Ibid., p. 192.

lation of Europe ... showed to the fate of the Jew is grounded in the general atomization within modern society, where the victimization of strangers evokes few or no responses.' And in an essay whose title itself has moral indifference as being 'the form of modern evil', Rainer C. Baum has written likewise of such indifference being 'deeply woven into the social fabric of modern life'. By focusing on the criminality of the SS, the Nuremberg trials created what Baum calls a 'false alibi' for the German people. The genocide was made possible because 'the vast majority simply did not care'. In the light of that experience, he suggests, we should realize how deeply laid are 'opportunities for amoral conduct' within the circumstances of modern life; how easy it is 'to adopt the role of the passive bystander'.[39] To return to Bauman on this point, a pressing need of our time, according to him, is a new ethics that would be commensurate with the conditions of modernity, 'an ethics of distance and distant consequences'. However: 'Whether such an ethics is a practical prospect is an altogether different matter'.[40]

This is the moral desideratum formulated in the measured tones of the social theorist where we have heard it formulated hitherto in other tones: of the uncomprehending question, the stern judgement, the passion and the solemnity of prayer. There was an anticipation of rage also, kindling at a poet's word. Now listen to this.

Somewhere there are people producing copy for Amnesty International and urgently appealing to the conscience of anyone they can reach, appealing to them to do something, not to turn away. 'Listen', they say, 'Can you hear the silence?' They mean of the dead in Rwanda, 'the silent dead

39. George M. Kren, 'The Holocaust as History', in Rosenberg and Myers, *Echoes from the Holocaust*, p. 38; and Rainer C. Baum, 'Holocaust: Moral Indifference as *the* Form of Modern Evil', ibid., pp. 57, 61, 84.
40. *Modernity and the Holocaust*, pp. 220–21.

in their thousands. Lolling in fields, floating in rivers, riding the rapids down into Lake Victoria.' But they mean another silence as well: 'Do you know what our deadliest enemy is? It's not the guns of vicious tyrants. It's the silence of good people ... If you don't speak out, why should anyone else? ... Do not be part of the killing silence.'[41] The writer of this may be familiar with a proposition that is attributed in differing versions to Edmund Burke: 'The one condition necessary for the triumph of evil is that good men do nothing.'[42]

'When our children were dying' – begins another Amnesty appeal – 'you did nothing to help. Now God help your children.' These are the words of an Iraqi Kurdish refugee, and they refer to the use of poison gas against the Kurds by the regime of Saddam Hussein.[43] They recall other words, words coming down from the Nazi period: not only (as they do obliquely) the closing lines of Primo Levi's 'Shemà'; but also a rueful and probably more famous observation by Martin Niemoller, known this, once again, in a number of different versions:[44]

> First they came for the Jews
> and I did not speak out
> because I was not a Jew.
> Then they came for the Communists
> and I did not speak out
> because I was not a Communist.

41. From Amnesty International appeal letter of June 1994, over the signature of Jo Wells (Africa Research Department).
42. As given in Ronnie S. Landau, *The Nazi Holocaust*, London 1992, p. 222. And cf. Angela Partington, ed., *The Oxford Dictionary of Quotations*, Oxford 1992, pp. 159–60.
43. This appeal, a copy of which is in my possession, appeared in a national newspaper, probably the *Guardian*, in late 1991. I have been unable to track down the issue.
44. In Schiff, *Holocaust Poetry*, p. 9. Other versions have the sequence differently, beginning with the Communists.

> Then they came for the trade unionists
> and I did not speak out
> because I was not a trade unionist.
> Then they came for me
> and there was no one left
> to speak out for me.

Whether or not the people drafting Amnesty International's material are directly familiar with the words of others which it echoes, they are in any case familiar with the meaning of the Holocaust precedent for the issues to which this material relates. 'Take a good look', they write under a photograph reminiscent in certain ways of photographs from that time; 'Don't ever say "I didn't know it was happening".' The picture is from Bosnia and is of prisoners in a Serbian-run prison camp: 'For God's sake get angry', the writers demand of us.[45] And then, 'Because we do nothing' they have put beneath another terrible picture, the picture of a young woman hanging by the neck from a tree.[46] And on a leaflet that it needs some resolve just to keep on reading, 'What will it take to make you cry out ... This? Or this? [and on the reverse side] This?' The leaflet urges us to cry out to help stop torture.[47]

This. Consider that it has been. Consider that it still is. How go on as normal after having seen it? How, even, go on as normal merely knowing about it? Forgive me, but here is what we are being told of in these Amnesty appeals. Of savage beatings, a man crucified, a girl raped to death. Of children as young as five tortured in front of their families, and parents tortured in front of their children. Of exhaust pipes used to burst people's lungs, water being forced into

45. *Guardian*, September 19 1992, p. 9.
46. From Amnesty International appeal letter of August 1995, over the signature of David Bull (Director, British Section).
47. Amnesty International appeal leaflet, undated (but in fact from late 1995; reissued during 1997).

their stomachs. Of women raped with bottles, with electric cattle prods, of children disfigured with hot irons. Of the gouging and the burning out of eyes, the cutting off of noses, ears, breasts, penises, the axing of limbs, the ripping out of tongues.[48] There is more, but I will stop. In his account of a symposium on torture held at Leiden University, Dr. Harold Hillman reports that the screams of the victims of torture are 'unimaginable'. He reports the view of one participant in the symposium, that 'people in free countries should show solidarity with those who suffer'. He wonders 'whether there could be more important causes than stopping torture'.[49] Helen Bamber, who set up and directs the Medical Foundation for the Care of Victims of Torture, says: 'Nothing saps people more than the fact that nobody cares'.[50]

However, 'this' . . . perhaps it is elsewhere. Perhaps and perhaps not; it depends on where you are. 'Successive British Governments have continued to permit sales of equipment used for torture to countries with appalling human rights records . . . The booming torture and cruelty business is worth millions a year to western firms, whose catalogues contain products ranging from medieval style thumb-cuffs and leg-irons to sophisticated electro-shock equipment.'[51] British governments, western firms, instruments of torture. In Britain today the membership of Amnesty International is something over one hundred thousand. This is in a population of fifty-eight million. Think, says Amnesty's publicity, what a million of us could do.[52] But the membership of Amnesty *world-wide* is about a million. And torture is used by more than sixty, perhaps by as many as a hundred, of the

48. All taken from the items cited at footnotes 43, 45 and 47 above.
49. Harold Hillman, 'The "Masters" of Torture', *AIBS Journal* (October/November 1992), pp. 13–14.
50. Mary Anne Fitzgerald, 'Coming Through Torture', *Guardian*, August 13 1992.
51. Amnesty advertisement, *Guardian*, March 16 1996, p. 13.
52. See the items given at footnotes 45 and 46 above.

world's governments.[53] Whether or not the critical ratio here – of Amnesty's members and supporters to everyone else – is significantly better than the ratio of those who were willing to help Jews in danger to that great majority of Europeans who stood by to their persecution and annihilation, it is not very impressive in view of the barbarities with which it co-exists. It is less impressive still when set against the consideration of how many people (world-wide) could do something to try to stop such barbarities, to put pressure on their governments to try to stop them, without any appreciable risk to their own lives and security.

If I focus on the horror of torture as challenging the inaction of all those who could act against it but do not, torture is, unhappily, not the only polar extremity – over against the comforts and security, sometimes the luxury, others enjoy – that challenges their inaction. Students and survivors of the Jewish tragedy draw the parallels, in this respect, with other such extremities: with genocide and mass hunger. We have touched in passing on one or two of the subsequent tragedies that have mocked the postwar rhetoric of 'Never again'. The list of them goes on being extended: from East Timor and Cambodia to Bosnia and Rwanda. As one writer has observed, it is doubtful whether the most important lessons of the Nazi period have been grasped even theoretically, but 'certainly they have not been *applied*, as attested by the alarming frequency of postwar instances of genocide [and] by the consistent failure of the United Nations to invoke its own Genocide Convention of 1948'. The same writer goes on to refer to the seeming 'indifference of the developed world in the face of starvation and misery of millions'.[54] Misery of millions is no exaggeration. Accord-

---

53. The figures are from Fitzgerald, 'Coming Through Torture'; Eric Hobsbawm, 'Barbarism: A User's Guide', *New Left Review* 206 (July/August 1994), p. 51; and enquiries to Amnesty International itself.
54. Landau, *The Nazi Holocaust*, p. 263.

ing to a recent report by the World Health Organization more than one-fifth of the world's population live in extreme poverty, and poverty is 'the leading cause of premature death and ill health across the planet'.[55]

We may return to what was our starting point here: to Poland and Warsaw and the words once more of Adina Szwajger, remembering the days in April 1943 when the Germans were burning the ghetto:

> And the people? On Krasinski Square [with the carousel], and on the streets generally? For me they all had one face, an empty one. Because it was all far away. Behind the wall. It just did not concern them. In the same way we are not really concerned about children dying from hunger in Biafra, Ethiopia, or in India.[56]

Yet it is not really so far away. For as Terrence Des Pres has written, 'The age-old belief in "the oneness of man" has become, in our time, a visible actuality – the result of war and mass murder, of world politics and the economic interdependence of classes and nations.'[57] It is not so far away even apart from this when there are people homeless on the streets of nearly all modern cities.

55. Chris Mihill, 'Fifth of world's people live in poverty', *Guardian*, May 2 1995.
56. *I Remember Nothing More*, p. 164.
57. Terrence Des Pres, *The Survivor: An Anatomy of Life in the Death Camps*, New York 1976, p. 44.

II A Different Kind of Contract

What has been the response of political philosophy to the Shoah? Put differently, where is there the political philosophy that has attempted to take the measure of this awful human disaster of the twentieth century? In fact, a political philosopher coming to the study of it may be surprised how little she will find in the way of serious and extended reflection on the subject from others of her calling, the notable counter-example of Hannah Arendt notwithstanding. There is a marked contrast between the situation within this ancient tradition of enquiry on the one hand, and the abundant materials we now have – and of which the previous section gives some small indication – that we owe to the disciplines of history, theology, literary criticism, the various social sciences, to the activities of dramatists, film-makers, novelists and poets, on the other. This is not to say there is no matter to be found which is pertinent to the distinctive domain of political philosophy in works about the Shoah produced outside that domain. There is such matter. The conventional boundaries are not clear-cut, and the attempt to come to terms with a calamity of such magnitude has reached right across them, no merely customary lines of intellectual division being able to contain, much less to exhaust, it. All the more surprising is it in these circumstances that political philosophers have so little addressed the event as being of significance for their concerns.

It will be said that the strong preoccupation within contemporary political thought with concepts of rights and of justice has itself been shaped to some large extent by a recognition of the moral disasters of our century, the destruction of the

Jews of Europe amongst them. This is doubtless true. But where in other areas of enquiry or 'representation' the sheer scale and the specificities – some would say, too, the terrible singularity – of this disaster have seemed to many to demand a particular attention and response, within political philosophy no similar need has been felt.

Normative theoretical conceptions not tested against the worst calamities of our time might be thought to be taking life more easily than they should. Theories of rights and justice which do not seriously measure themselves against the realities of violation – violation of the norms about which they theorize, violation of the lives of human beings – and do not seriously measure themselves against the factors conducive to such violation, might be reckoned by this failure to be lacking in an important way.

What, to get to the point now, are the implications for normative political theory of the bystander phenomenon: that is, of the depressing but widespread fact that so many people do not come to the aid of others under attack, whether fellow citizens or merely other human beings, and also do not come to the aid of them in dire need or great distress? This question is posed, of course, not only by the catastrophe that overtook Europe's Jews while much of the world remained unmoved, but also by other sufferings past and present. But in any event that catastrophe, the stain of it covering a continent, poses the question with especial clarity. As the historian Yehuda Bauer has said in this connection, expressing it as an issue of 'basic morality':

> We have much to learn yet about the Holocaust in this, as well as in other, areas of inquiry. But as we all know, the question is no less important than the answer. We are asking about the human response to human tragedy, about the feeling of community between groups and individuals ... The Holocaust is a touchstone of such inquiry.[58]

58. Yehuda Bauer, *The Holocaust in Historical Perspective*, Seattle 1978, pp. 91–2.

The violation of some by others, their public humiliation, dispossession, deportation, enslavement, torture, murder, in the sight, or with the knowledge, of many more others who could but do not act to stop it, who stand by, look on or look away – these are the poles of extremity from which we begin. As we have seen in the previous section, the moral tension, so to put it, that they conjointly establish, is widely registered in the literature of the Holocaust. The moral tension set up between the enormous sufferings of some people and the blank inaction of others in response is registered in the many different genres and idioms of which that extensive literature is now composed. I want to re-express the same thing in the language of political theory, adapting an old notion from within this tradition of discourse for the purpose: I shall formulate it in terms of the idea of a contract, but a contract of a rather different kind.

This is not the 'social' contract in its most familiar meaning, as given here in two general introductory surveys of the idea: according to which 'a social contract theory is a theory in which a contract is used to justify and/or to set limits to political authority, or ... in which political obligation is analysed as a contractual obligation'; or in which the central idea is 'that legitimate government is the artificial product of the voluntary agreement of free moral agents'.[59] My own focus is not upon political obligation or legitimate government.

It differs, further, from dominant uses of the social contract idea, both classical and contemporary, in the following two ways. First, the contract I shall speak of is not a contract of social or political *origin*, not one, that is, belonging to the past, whether really or hypothetically; and nor is it conceived from some wholly conjectural starting point, as with the

59. Michael Lessnoff, *Social Contract*, London 1986, p. 2; and Patrick Riley, 'social contract', in David Miller, ed., *The Blackwell Encyclopaedia of Political Thought*, Oxford 1987, p. 478.

'original position' in the theory of John Rawls. Although it is in a certain manner an imputed contract, it is one, as I shall argue, that can be read from the realities of our time, taken this in the large sense so as to include, let us say, the century. (It is imputable to some past time or condition only in so far as that may have been characterized by pertinently similar realities; and otherwise it is not.) Second, the argument I shall offer for the existence of this contract does not, therefore, rest on any state of being temporally or logically prior to the contract itself. It does not rest on any construct like the 'state of nature' or the Rawlsian 'original position'. And it is not burdened, consequently, with all the well-known problems attending constructs of this sort, to do with what should be put into the prior state, and what should be left out of it; and with how to settle this question in a way that does not itself arbitrarily generate some favoured conclusion or other of the thinker whose construct it is. We deal with the agents, in other words, with the parties to the contract, pretty much as they are, and not as abstracted from their real conditions of life.

Here is the core idea. If you do not come to the aid of others who are under grave assault, in acute danger or crying need, you cannot reasonably expect others to come to your aid in similar emergency; you cannot consider them so obligated to you. Other people, equally, unmoved by the emergencies of others, cannot reasonably expect to be helped in deep trouble themselves, or consider others obligated to help them. I call this *the contract of mutual indifference.* I propose it reluctantly, go into it hoping to be able to come out of it on the other side.

The case for the reality of this contract may be made as follows. Consider, as an 'ideal type' or limit position, a world in which nobody ever comes to the aid of anyone else under grave assault or cognate misfortune, and in which there are plenty of instances of that. Even though no formal agreement had been made between the individuals of this world to the effect that they owed one another, under threat or misfortune, nothing in the way of aid or care, the case for imputing such an agreement to them would be compelling. For, given their bystanding dispositions, no one could reasonably entertain a contrary expectation towards the generality of his fellows: along the lines, for example, 'even though I shall do nothing for others very unfortunately placed myself, nevertheless I think they would be obliged to help me and I shall look forward to their help should I ever need it.' No one could persuasively defend such an expectation to other people; not, at least, without the presupposition of some special and unequal relationship of obligation privileging himself, of a type which I intend simply to discount here.

Now, this limit position of mutual indifference is not some *other*, temporally prior, state of being, nor is it a purely hypothetical construct set behind a 'veil': behind a screen of abstraction which separates us from what we know or what we are. It is rather a model of the world which we really inhabit, although it is exaggerated – or, better perhaps, reduced – by omission of such mutually assisting behaviour in dire misfortune as there is. Still, it is a model of our world. The state of affairs described by this contract of mutual indifference is close enough to the actual state of affairs in our world as to portray accurately the relations generally prevailing between most of the people in it. So clear, it seems to me, is the case that it does accurately portray these relations that certain 'boundary' questions and lines of possible counter-argument can be more easily handled than they otherwise could, a degree of fuzziness in the way we handle them being not just acceptable, but even apt.

Thus, first, what is the extent of misfortune or trouble creating a presumption of the need for aid, and short of (less than) which we would be able to feel satisfied that the world under consideration was not marked by undue indifference even though everyone simply went their own care-free way? And, assuming some answer to this question, what is the extent of the helping response from any individual that would represent a sufficiency, morally speaking, and what the social spread of sufficient responses that would enable us to feel, once again, satisfied that a general unconcern over the plight of others did not prevail? I offer no answers to these two questions. With the amount and the extremes of what there actually is in the world of brutal oppression, genocide, torture, famine and the rest, the numbers of people not directly affected by it who do nothing at all, next to nothing, or very little indeed to oppose or remedy it, is so large as to put the issue beyond doubt that we are on the wrong side by far of what the relevant lines of moral demarcation ought to be.

Second, the suggestion can be just as quickly dealt with that there is in fact nothing (most) people can do about it all. This would be a version of the 'ought implies can' thesis and might be elaborated so. Given the nature of the evils under consideration, evils that are very great, often locked into institutional networks or social and political systems difficult to transform or overturn, and sometimes also geographically distant from the people who come to know about them as evils, there is nothing effective they can do to oppose them. The view that they do too little is therefore misconceived. However, they *can* do *something*. It is a merely banal point that many small responses can add up to a great response, and the observation is also common that responses of protest against injustice and needless suffering tend to encourage other similar responses, while conversely silence, unconcern, complicity and the like feed upon themselves, they feed the same dispositions in others. So people can certainly do something.

Reflecting on one of the best counter-examples we have to the model of any wholly generalized indifference – I mean the rescue of the Jews of Denmark – a minister of the Danish Church who was himself involved in that collective act has written: 'No protest against injustice and brutality is ever made altogether in vain'.[60] Hannah Arendt likewise, speaking of acts of non-compliance with Nazi criminality, says that nothing in that regard 'can ever be "practically useless", at least, not in the long run.'[61] Needless to say, these two comments concern political circumstances rather more testing than many of the subjects of the contract I here hypothesize typically have to face. Whether or not the comments are literally true, true for every single conceivable case of protest at, or non-compliance with, grave wrong, their general truth is surely undeniable.

I anticipate now, third, the objection that no one can reasonably be expected to give their lives entirely to helping others. A thought of this kind was expressed by Barrington Moore: 'to demand that all human beings devote absolutely all of their energies to eliminating evil and injustice is in itself somehow mean-spirited, twisted, and narrow'. Moore makes reference in this context to the existence of 'other values'; he mentions specifically 'scientific and artistic effort that [does] not serve immediately visible social ends'.[62] Richard Rorty has urged, in like manner, that we do not have to choose between 'self-creation and justice, private perfection and human solidarity'. He says we should treat the demands of each as being equally valid.[63] And other philosophers as well advise against setting the demands of social morality so high that the personal projects of the individual, or her sense of what is essential to her own

60. Poul Borchsenius, 'Aspects of the Rescue of Danish Jews', *Wiener Library Bulletin* 22/4, New Series 13 (Autumn 1968), pp. 36–40.
61. Hannah Arendt, *Eichmann in Jerusalem*, London 1977, pp. 232–3.
62. Barrington Moore Jr, *Reflections on the Causes of Human Misery*, London 1972, p. 78.
63. Richard Rorty, *Contingency, Irony, and Solidarity*, Cambridge 1989, pp. xiii–xv.

integrity, are brought to nothing or very little beside them. In the light of this kind of concern, the objection might be offered, then, that it is unreasonable to pitch the level of self-sacrifice on behalf of others too high.

Indeed. It is an exacting and joyless philosophy that would do that. But I have not yet pitched the level at any determinate height. Suppose we were to say – to the view that people should not be asked to give up their whole lives, all their time, for the sake of others – that they might be asked to give up twenty-five, or twenty, or even ten per cent only of their *free* time (and some substantial proportion of their disposable income) to the end of trying to stop torture, deal with famine and so on. Would this be excessively high? Assuming for the moment the answer is no, how much do most people do even so measured? In fact, how little do they do. To the objection in any case that too much should not be demanded, one could just demand less: more than nothing where that is appropriate, more than a very little where this is. It would cover for much. As for those situations where a very great deal more, at the limit a person's freedom or life, has to be given or risked to help someone else, I venture nothing about this for the time being, save that the cases of it would be fewer than they are the less moral indifference there was towards the sufferings of others.

Fourth, it may be said that by speaking in the very general way I do about grave assault, acute danger and crying need, about genocide, torture, famine, I imply an impossibly strenuous burden of mutual obligation on everyone, in virtue of the amount of what there is in the world of these sorts of thing. However, *you* don't have to act against all of it. This would indeed create an impossible burden of obligation. The presumption negatively carried by the contract of mutual indifference is only that people all need to act against some of it.

Not to do anything at all, or to do extremely little, when

confronted with vast suffering and injustice, invites the question as to what basis you would have to appeal to the help of others should the need for this arise. You live, say, a life more or less wholly concerned with private, self-regarding ends and the ends of very closely related others – of your family, your intimates – in the shadow of widespread human catastrophe. You answer the question just lately posed, answer it in what you say or by how you live, with the view that even ten per cent of your free time (and disposable income) is too much to give, judged against the cries of the tortured and the look in the eyes of the destitute. How could you reasonably expect the help of others if anything similar, or even much less severe but bad enough, were to befall you?

Perhaps, though, I simplify too much. Perhaps I simplify too much in treating the model of mutual indifference, from which I derive the contract of that same designation, as an acceptably close approximation to the world in which we live. Naturally, like all models this one does simplify in various ways. But does it do so in ways inappropriate to the issues under discussion? I want now to consider four – later I shall take up a few other – possible suggestions as to why the model may be thought to simplify in ways that are illegitimate.

First, the suggestion might be made that it does not give an accurate picture of the general (worldly) state of affairs because the relationship of mutual indifference is precisely not a universal one. There exist what can be called subgroups of mutual concern and care. These may be families, groups of friends, communities based on neighbourhood or work-place, or on common ethnic, national or religious identifi-cation, and so forth. Few people in grave misfortune are altogether alone. This is true. However, I have not said that the relation of mutual indifference is a universal one; only that it is general. The model fits the *general* state of affairs in the world in the sense of holding with respect to the vast majority of inter-individual relations in it. This is not, in my view, a restriction that undermines the overall thesis. For subgroups of mutual concern and care do not meet the problem of grave assault, acute danger and crying need. Or rather if they do, it is a matter of luck. People went to their deaths at Auschwitz and Treblinka, notwithstanding that there were some others who cared about them. Whole communities were slaughtered in the forests of eastern Europe, as more recently they have been brutally violated and dispersed in former Yugoslavia, despite the fact that the individuals composing these communities were not entirely alone. In face of the common size of such crises in the modern world, the dangers and misfortunes we are talking about can sink any person despite the subgroup he may belong to, and they can sink any subgroup as well, in a context of generalized indifference.

The same type of response I think meets the suggestion of a second putative oversimplification. The suggestion would be to the effect that duties of extensive aid and care are more widely recognized by individuals than my model allows, but they are, in some sort, delegated by them to states and governments. They are delegated to states and governments as being the bodies able most effectively to discharge them. To this suggestion I say: that states and governments are themselves often the very source of the calamities we are talking about and therefore cannot be relied upon as the guarantors (of aid) of last resort; that in plain view of such calamities, other states and governments than the offending ones regularly stand by and do nothing or very little, and therefore, once again, cannot be so relied upon; and that the supposition would seem to be a sound one that in this matter governments may not be much better, much more responsive to the disasters of others whether at home or abroad, than the generality of their active citizens is able to make them. On all these counts the responsibility of the individual human being for the fate of other human beings cannot be simply shifted on to the institutions of government.

Third, it may be said that I assume in all this a level of awareness about situations of moral extremity which is much exaggerated; I assume it by speaking as though all who are inactive in response to instances of moral extremity in some sense *decide* to be inactive. If they are not aware, however, of any such instances, of situations thought to call for opposing or remedial action on their part, they cannot fairly be seen in this way, as wilfully indifferent, bystanders by intent. This is the plea of ignorance: they do not know. How much weight can it really be given? There may be people in the world fortunate enough never to come within 'knowing-distance' of any of the human disasters it so readily accommodates, but for sufficient millions of others, certainly many more than those, it is not the case. The evidence of human disaster is everywhere available. The echoes of it are, in contemporary conditions of the flow and the active diffusion of information, nearly impossible to escape for any significant length of time. Not to know or not to know enough, you have to turn aside, you have resolutely to ignore the signals of distress that come your way. In these circumstances the plea of a lack of knowledge is uncompelling. It treats as an involuntary state what is itself in fact a choice. To adapt the judgement of one scholar concerning this same plea by many Germans after 1945 with respect to the fate of the Jews: those who are unaware know enough to know that they prefer not to know any more.[64]

The fourth suggestion I anticipate is of an oversimplifying assumption of a rather different kind. It is that the picture of

64. See David Bankier, 'The Germans and the Holocaust: What Did They Know?', *Yad Vashem Studies* 20 (1990), p. 98. Bankier's conclusion: 'They knew enough to know that it was better not to know more.'

a morally more desirable state of affairs critically implied here by the mutual indifference argument is just plain psychologically unrealistic. This picture may be held to be unrealistic because the bonds of reciprocal concern and mutual aid can only ever be relatively small-scale; because it is simply our nature as a species to pursue our *own* goals to the very considerable extent that rules out any attitude of even moderately energetic stranger-oriented concern; because, to cite Primo Levi again (but is this in another voice?), 'if we had to and were able to suffer the sufferings of everyone, we could not live. Perhaps the dreadful gift of pity for the many is granted only to saints'.[65]

One line of response would be to say that we know from enough human examples of other-regarding effort that more of such effort is possible for people than most of them, in conditions of mutual indifference, now give. What might be possible in general, consequently, is a matter for exploration and practical advocacy and initiative. Rather less than universal saintliness would be needed significantly to improve the world, and therefore we should not fix the ideal so low as to obstruct the prospects of such improvement. Another, more pessimistic line of response, however, would be to concede that the picture of a morally better state of affairs *is* psychologically unrealistic: to accept that, whatever may be possible for individuals in principle, for the large majority of them it is simply unlikely that they would ever be willing to give much consideration to the misfortunes of others in relation to their own preoccupations and enjoyments. But I do not see how this helps to avoid the conclusion – the conclusion of the contract of mutual indifference. If it is unrealistic to expect much of people by way of mutual aid in situations of great menace or misfortune, then others should not perhaps

65. Primo Levi, *The Drowned and the Saved*, London 1989, pp. 39–40.

expect such aid of you. But how, confirming this pessimistic expectation, can you reasonably expect any aid from them?

I now approach a critical juncture in the argument. I shall come to it by way of registering a necessary clarification. It is no part of the case I put forward to argue that people who do nothing in face of the terrible misfortunes of others *deserve* to suffer some equivalent misfortune themselves, or that it would be good if they did. The point is only that, doing nothing for others, they cannot reasonably expect to be helped in extremity themselves or consider others under obligation to help them. It is as though they agree by their own inaction to forego any expectation of help they might otherwise entertain. They waive any right to help they might be thought to possess.

However, suppose that, whatever people may feel able to expect, whatever they have agreed to or are taken on account of their conduct to have agreed to, they do have precisely a right in this matter, a right to aid in dire emergency, and others a corresponding obligation to come to their aid; and suppose that there is no contract which can loosen this bond, the right to help in such circumstances being inalienable. Let me say that I find this supposition, for my own part, of strong appeal. If no one deserves to suffer the sort of afflictions we are talking about here – the brutal violations, barbarous cruelties, the extremes of impoverishment and need – it is because these are abominations. They ought to be intolerable within the human community. One way of giving expression to the moral sense that they ought to be is by the hypothesis of a right to be helped in emergency and of a correlative duty to bring aid.

One might linger now in an attempt to judge the strength of this moral sense, on the one hand, against the persuasive power attaching to reciprocal agreement and expectation, on the other. Thus how, it might be asked, can we discount considerations of reciprocity in the present context if we are to give weight to a principle of moral equality? That you owe someone help in distress no matter what her derelictions towards you and others may be – or, in terms of the contract of mutual indifference, that you owe her it though she releases you by implicit agreement in never being prepared to help anyone herself – would seem to underwrite a species of moral privilege. It is a privilege for the bystander: to do what she will without forfeit, to be supported in adversity although she herself is not prepared to give any comparable support. But, then again, perhaps it is exactly so: that grave, remediable suffering brings with it, despite everything, the 'privilege' of help from others. I do not intend to dwell upon how we might adjudicate the respective strengths of these competing moral intuitions, much less to explore how the intuitions could be integrated into alternative moral theories to be adjudicated on that basis.

I will simply say that there is a crucial sense in which the contract has priority over the right; it is of a practical moral import that defeats it. For if by agreement people just do as a matter of practice generally waive any putative right to aid in emergency, if they mutually discount by their conduct any duty to bring aid, the right to aid is rendered thereby nuga-tory. It is as if we did not have one; in effect we do not have one. Some might *feel* there is such a right. Others might put themselves to the task of deriving it from a well-fashioned, more or less elaborate moral theory. For yet others it might be a point of religious faith and in need of no theoretical derivation that a human being is not to be left to suffer in dreadful ways when others can intervene to prevent this. Still, if people do mutually agree willy-nilly not to respect it, the right has no force. There is no firmer protection for the values governing the interaction of human beings than the moral cultures and practices that obtain between them. Invoke as we may – against their reciprocal agreements – the will of God, or moral intuition, or the power of philosophical reasoning, the contract of mutual indifference can just remain in place, its normativity while it prevails defying any better one.

There is a more serious consequence still. This conclusion touches not only any hypothetical right to receive help in emergency, which would be a right, obviously, to positive action or provision by other people. It touches those rights also called 'negative': rights to be left alone by others, not to be harmed, not to be interfered with when pursuing one's legitimate ends. We cleave as we do to such rights because the world is a dangerous place. It is a lot more dangerous for some than it is for others, but there is nevertheless a shared and ineradicable vulnerability of persons, vulnerability to violation by other persons. In a wholly benign and unmenacing world these rights against violation would not matter, at any rate not to the same extent or in the same way. In the world as it is they do matter; violations are to be expected and regularly happen. But in so far as a contract of mutual indifference prevails, the negative rights, too, become in effect null. They are only as good as the protection people generally will put behind them. Giving them no protection yourself by the way you live, by omitting to do anything (much) to help remedy the violations of negative right that you know about, you may still find yourself lucky enough to get remedy when a negative right of your own is breached. But without special pleading what case could you make why others *owed* it to you to protect your negative rights if you had taken no care at all for theirs?

It follows that unless we make an effort on behalf of others under grave assault or in acute danger, an effort – and a moderately strenuous one at least – to secure their rights, in effect we have no rights ourselves. Or, to put it otherwise, if we do not respect a strong positive obligation to bring aid, we throw away even the most minimal of negative rights. Without a duty to help there are effectively no rights against harm. We are then alone and most people owe us nothing in conditions of disaster for us.

Everyone alone. Even as the bearers of notional rights. Plunged into danger or misfortune as they always may be, they will find that by way of the contract of mutual indifference others generally are under no obligation to them, and their rights merely notional indeed, emptied by that contract of overriding normative force.

I cannot say that he intended exactly this thought but I believe the following passage from Primo Levi reflects something of it. The passage concerns Chaim Rumkowski, a notorious figure from amongst the Jewish ghetto leaderships in Nazi-occupied Poland, a man who took collaboration with the oppressor in the hope of consequential benefit about as far as it can go, without thereby avoiding the fate of the rest of his people. Levi writes of him:

> [W]e are all mirrored in Rumkowski, his ambiguity is ours ... and his miserable tinsel trappings the distorted image of our symbols of social prestige ... Like Rumkowski, we too are so dazzled by power and money as to forget our essential fragility, forget that all of us are in the ghetto, that the ghetto is fenced in, that beyond the fence stand the lords of death, and not far away the train is waiting.[66]

A similar thought receives expression in the searing pages of Jean Améry. Améry speaks of the 'moral truth' by which, as a victim of Nazi persecution, he was held forever captive; one learned through the experience of persecution as 'an extreme *loneliness*', leading to permanent loss of trust in the world.[67]

(Here I must interrupt the passage of exposition and argument. Whenever I have reached the present point,

66. Primo Levi, *Moments of Reprieve*, London 1986, p. 172.
67. Jean Améry, *At the Mind's Limits*, New York 1990, p. 70. And cf. pp. 28, 40, 96.

whether vaguely as a still nebulous idea, or more clearly as a thesis in process of taking formal shape, from the day of that journey to Headingley cricket ground when the idea first occurred to me, up to this moment in composition, I have been seized with a strong feeling of discomfort. It is not due just to the bleakness of the conclusion. Having gone over this now many times, I am persuaded of its necessity on some level: its necessity as formulating, without easy solace, one of the realities so often given voice to by the victims, even if in another idiom than theirs. The sensation comes rather, so far as I can claim to understand it, from articulating the moral logic of this reality, from putting myself in the position of propounding it. From making myself its spokesman. The feeling of discomfort connects, I believe, to an emotion which I shall be discussing later, in Section III of this essay. Surely one ought to protest such a moral logic and not propound it, not seek to persuade others of its force. Of course. One can protest it and one must. But a protest uninformed of the power of what it protests against is not always the most effective kind. In what follows, I go on to see if the moral logic of the contract of mutual indifference is softened at all, mitigated, by considerations I have so far left to one side. I acknowledge that it is. But I urge, without attempt to rebut them, that these considerations leave the offending logic too much in place. It is a logic that needs to be more than merely mitigated.)

Earlier, I anticipated some suggestions to the effect that the model of mutual indifference I propose is too simplified vis-à-vis the world it purports to depict, and I tried to deal with these suggestions as best I could, arguing that none of them substantially undermined the case being put forward. I want now to consider three further such suggestions. With respect to them, by contrast, I will recognize that the case is in need of qualification.

First, there are people who live dedicated lives of other-regarding concern and action, and there are people also who, though doing much less, give some significant part of their time and energies in the same direction. Without stopping to estimate, much less to investigate, what the numbers or proportion of both sorts of people might be in one context or another (national, situational or whatever), I nevertheless do want to insist that, appearances to the contrary in this essay notwithstanding, I have no wish to minimize or marginalize the existence and importance of such people and what they do. I have elsewhere focused indeed on one remarkable example of their kind, in the context of the Holocaust itself, examining what it was that moved the rescuers of Jews in Nazi Europe to act as they did.[68] There is in any event a wide gradation amongst people who come to the aid of others: from those we may call saints or moral heroes, on the one hand, to the many impelled by ordinary sympathy or virtue to help on some more or less modest scale, on the other. They constitute, all of them, the nucleus of another moral universe than the one defined by the contract here under discussion. The question that is now posed by them is: can they be integrated within the schema of this contract? Or are they exempt from it, and people therefore generally obligated at least to *them* – to come to their aid in need because of what they do or have done? And then, how *much* does one have to have done to fall into this category?

Second, in the abstraction of mere 'individuals' and of the contract by which they are brought into relation, we have up to now overlooked (in a manner often thought to be characteristic of liberal political theory) those social factors, or structures, that result in different people being differently placed: in better positions or worse, with greater or lesser resources, with more and less available time, for coming to

68. See my *Solidarity in the Conversation of Humankind*, London 1995, chapter 1.

the aid of others. Once one takes account of real inequalities, of economic exploitation and various types of deprivation or oppression, one is bound to recognize that some will be more advantaged than others in their capacity to offer aid, to act in protest, to contribute time and effort to opposing injustice. At the limit, it follows from the very nature of the problem being addressed that some people, some or much or all of the time, will be pretty well disqualified by the extremity of their own situation from being able to help other people, except perhaps in the smallest of ways. How, in turn, are these factors to be brought under the conception of the contract of mutual indifference? What is the 'threshold of well-being', so to put it, above which a person should be expected to be willing to make a notable effort on behalf of others in danger or distress? And ought we to sketch a sliding scale of other-regarding obligations, set according to the relative advantage or capacity of potential helpers? Are we to take any account, in that case, of the psychological and ideological influences that will render many who are in the very best of positions to do something for others unwilling to put themselves to the cost of it?

Third, it might be said that what I proffer as a general contract lacks one of the pertinent features of such a contract. It lacks the feature of universalized reciprocity that would be needed for it to be thought of as holding effectively between all the individuals involved. I shall explain. The contract of mutual indifference may be presented as having something like this form: 'in exchange for being released by you from any putative duty or expectation calling upon me to come to your aid in distress, I similarly release you'. The point of this way of putting it, however, of putting it in the form of a bilateral agreement, is one of *justification*. It draws attention to the unreasonableness, other things equal, of someone's trying to claim different – that they alone should be released from an obligation to help, but not anyone else.

It is certainly not the point of the idea of the contract of mutual indifference to suggest that we ought to think of issues of mutual support and assistance in terms of an enormously large number of bilateral contracts, such that I can only expect aid from those whom I myself have helped, and they likewise; or such that I ought to be willing to help this particular person under attack in the rather unlikely hope that, should I ever be attacked myself, he might be on hand and willing to help me in return; and so forth. The matter here is not about strict one-to-one reciprocity. Relationships are to be thought of, not as bilateral and direct, but as representative, standardized; as brought under the idea of relationships of a characteristic type. If people, very generally, came to the aid of endangered others, they would be in a position to expect others to come to theirs. If *in general* they do not, then they are not in a position, morally, to expect that. Morally, they are on their own, whatever may transpire for them in fact.[69]

Now, at this juncture it might be expected that I would attempt to face and respond to these various considerations. I would seek to show by a series of more or less elaborate counter-arguments how they are not of any great consequence for my case. I would try to diminish their force. But I am not going to do this, and the reasons why I am not have already been partly stated in setting out the considerations themselves. I have no wish to diminish the place or the weight of helping and other altruistic behaviour in the world as it is. On the contrary, it should be celebrated, each episode and particle of it cherished, as the nucleus and possible harbinger of an alternative world, one grown at last beyond the acceptance of atrocity. Nor would I enter on a discourse that risked belittling the extent to which anyone

69. I am grateful to Vittorio Bufacchi for discussion of the matter raised in these last two paragraphs.

was restrained from helping behaviour by their own material hardships and oppressions. The purpose in hand, after all, is to highlight how just such hardships and oppressions are too much tolerated by those in a position to oppose them, and so it will not be sensible in the next breath to make light of the identical thing. I have no interest, finally, in straining to show that the contract of mutual indifference is more nearly like an actual plurality of bilateral agreements, setting up a situation of direct and universalized reciprocity, than it is intended to be. It is not that. It is a loose device: serving merely to approximate to real relationships that are pervasive.

Readers can make of this what they will. Some, perhaps, may draw enough comfort from the above qualifying considerations to reckon the whole idea of the contract I hypothesize undone. Others may think, like me, that it still captures a moral reality, that of the dominant pattern of relationships, even once the qualifications are taken into account. This is, anyway, what I do propose: that it captures, and all too well, a brutal moral reality. I offer one more thought towards this unpalatable conclusion.

The reckoning is skewed. The reckoning, that is to say, of the extent of indifference and inaction in face of the horrors perpetrated on other human beings, as against what we like to think of as 'normality': people behaving humanely, generously to a degree, sympathizing, helping, and so on. It is skewed, in intellect and emotion, by one of the very dispositions that contributes to the phenomenon of standing by itself, standing by and doing nothing when others are violated or when they suffer or perish for want of necessities. For how many people simply shut this out, as much as they can or most of the time? To engrave it on your heart, as Primo Levi appeals to us to do in his 'Shemà', is not easy. Like the bystander who turns away – or runs away – because she cannot bear to look, the mind, if not universally then at least commonly, finds it hard to cope with focusing on great cruelty or horror.[70] It turns away to pursue the ends of life. But then how *present* to it can the extent and place of those evils in the general scheme of things be? And how present to it the extent of the tolerance of them? There is a kind of circle here, the normal consciousness not easily able to grasp the full weight of horror in the world by virtue of not thinking about it too much.

For the realities can be unbearable. Whatever they may be to have to experience, for many of us they are unbearable even to think about. To be confronted by those images. The enjoyment of mass murder, by the murderers, by spectators. Or mere casualness towards it, a man idly chatting to his companion while others are made to dig their own graves. To read about torture. (To this day I remember the exact time and place when, as a child, I first became aware of its existence. I remember the detail that most sickened me.) How little of this would there have to be for the living comfortably with it by others to be itself an outrage? And how much of it there is. Since thinking about it is for many of us unbearable, however, we mostly do not. And then the reckoning is that much easier that the space of moral indifference is maybe not so large.

But the truth we discern here is another. It is that the moral reality I attempt to encapsulate in the contract of mutual indifference is ... *unbearable*. These mechanisms of denial themselves say it. It is unbearable that people should be made to suffer in terrible ways. So it gets shut out. But if it is unbearable that they should be made to, it is unbearable also that they are left to. And the more it is shut out, the more they are. But the less well-placed people then are to perceive the coexistence of the evil with, its adjacency to,

---

70. On running away, see the testimony reported in Lawrence L. Langer, *Holocaust Testimonies*, New Haven 1991, pp. 29–32.

their own lives. The less well-placed they are to estimate the extent of the 'leaving-to', the wide tolerance there is towards the misery of others.

Under the sign of a different moral reality, the duty would be to take the pain of thinking about these things. It would be to take it enough to feel obliged to act against them. I shall say something more about that in the next section. I want to conclude this one by bringing it back to the point with which I began it: to the near silence there has been about the Shoah within mainstream political philosophy, by contrast with the attention it has received in other areas of intellectual enquiry.

Theodor Adorno has put forward the view that a thinking which does not measure itself against extremity is 'in the nature of the musical accompaniment with which the SS liked to drown out the screams of its victims'.[71] This view seems to me rather overstated, but still, it contains an important point. One of the more momentous literatures of our century is the literature of the survivors, testimony to the scarcely thinkable that must nevertheless be thought. Large and in its way individualized as it may be, uneven as it also is, since not everyone writes with the illuminating perception of a Primo Levi, the evocative power of a Charlotte Delbo, the lucid, unsparing harshness of a Jean Améry, this literature testifies, all the same, to a common understanding. The voices composing it call attention to the lesson they them-selves know at so great a cost. Whether in hope, that this lesson will be learned, or – as time has worn on – more disconsolately because it has not been, they appeal to others to listen. A political philosophy that does not meet the demands bequeathed by this literature of testimony is not abreast of its specific tasks in its time.

I brush aside the idea that there are no such specific tasks.

71. Theodor Adorno, *Negative Dialectics*, London 1973, p. 365.

True, there are bodies of political thought that will not recognize as obliging them the sort of thing I have in mind. No matter. It leaves more than enough: a vast array of contemporary thinking broadly progressive in intent – liberal, radical, socialist, other – whose theories of justice and rights, visions of utopia or the good or well-ordered society, notions of plural identity and deliberative democracy, project an amelioration of the world. They need to have at their centre, such theories and visions and notions, but generally they do not, a positive universal right to aid and the universal obligation to bring it. It should be there as the queen of all the virtues – not to remain a bystander in the face of preventable or remediable suffering. Without this the rest is made nugatory. It becomes a feeble aspiration, however benign, unwilling to attend to its own requirements of consistency, its own indispensable conditions of possibility *qua* projected alternative.

Some will perhaps hear here the echo of a famous formula concerning agency. 'The point is to change it' and so forth. However, this is not that, as important as that is. For it is not only a matter of calling the theory or thinker to attend to the needs of the world beyond the theory. It speaks to the internal coherence of the theory itself. It speaks to its inner inadequacy if it does not contain – emphatically, integrally, as a thread binding together all its norms, assumptions and expectations – the duty to bring aid. This is an essential component, not just *some other* question, beyond the theory or subordinate within it. Without this component, the theory risks being a nullity before the horrors of brute fact that continue their lethal work. Theories of rights, conceptions of justice, adumbrations of feasible utopia, must be insufficient when they do not encompass the requirement of a pervasive moral culture of mutual aid. An idea of mandatory care is their supreme exigency.

III The Duty to Bring Aid

There is an aspect of the unconditional in the duty to come to the help of people in danger. This has about it the pull of an irresistible demand. A sense of its unconditionality suffuses the literature of catastrophe; it breaks forth there again and again. Let us look for it first in what may appear the least likely of places: among those whom one might think not in a good position to help, or not in any position to.

In Zygmunt Bauman's book, the story is cited of a Polish family that offered to hide a Jewish friend during the German occupation but declined to take in his three sisters, more obviously Jewish in speech and appearance than he was. But the friend would not be saved alone. The writer here, who learned of this episode from another member of the family, reports:

> Had the decision of my family been different, there were nine chances to one that we would all be shot. The probability that our friend and his sisters would survive in those conditions was perhaps smaller still. And yet the person telling me this family drama and repeating 'What could we do, there was nothing we could do!', did not look me in the eyes. He sensed I felt a lie, though all the facts were true.[72]

Speaking of circumstances even more directly threatening than these, one Dora Rosenboim names the emotion which was this man's in being unable to look his interlocutor in the eyes. According to Rosenboim's testimony, in a village near Lodz in 1942, during the Purim festival, the Gestapo ordered

72. Cited in Bauman, *Modernity and the Holocaust*, pp. 201–2.

ten young Jews hanged by the Jewish police, with the rest of
the community forced out of their houses to watch.

> Many women fainted seeing the terrible and horrible sight, how ten
> of our brothers were writhing on the gallows. Our faces were
> ashamed and our hearts ached, but we could not help ourselves.[73]

Prisoners at Auschwitz were also forced to be present at
hangings. Primo Levi tells of one of these; and of his feeling
afterwards of being 'oppressed by shame'.[74] And it is Levi
who, as not uncommonly in this domain, has put that feeling
into the form of a more general and troubling wisdom for
his readers. I shall quote him at length since what he has to
say about shame bears upon our theme.

Levi writes of the moment of liberation for himself and
some other prisoners left behind at the evacuation of Auschwitz. He describes how the Russian soldiers coming upon
him and his group seemed overtaken by 'a confused
restraint' at the sight before them.

> It was the same shame which we knew so well, which submerged us
> after the selections, and every time we had to witness or undergo an
> outrage: the shame that the Germans never knew, the shame which
> the just man experiences when confronted by a crime committed by
> another, and he feels remorse because of its existence, because of
> its having been irrevocably introduced into the world of existing
> things, and because his will has proven nonexistent or feeble and
> was incapable of putting up a good defence.[75]

The act of witnessing. It is perhaps only an accident of
expression but Dora Rosenboim says: our *faces* were ashamed.
That is where it is, in the face. Primary point of interchange

---

73. See Martin Gilbert, *The Holocaust: The Jewish Tragedy*, p. 299.
74. Primo Levi, *If This is a Man and The Truce*, London 1987, pp. 154–6.
75. *The Drowned and the Saved*, p. 54. Levi is here quoting a passage from his own
earlier memoir of liberation. See *If This is a Man and The Truce*, p. 188.

between the world and the self. To see such a thing. To have to face it. And to be unable to look another in the eyes. Seeing, a mode of and common metaphor for knowing. Averting one's face, a way not to know. This has, consequently, more sources than one. Not only the inability to bear what you might see should you carry on looking, but another avoidance as well: shame. The shame of seeing and not acting. And whatever the conditions and the risks – although, to be sure, the greater the risks, the less 'genuine' the cause for shame, as we are bound on some level also to feel. But is it not conversely then, too? And the shame proper to humanity incalculable?

Levi in fact goes on to speak of such 'another vaster shame, the shame of the world'. Invoking John Donne, he speaks about those who, like the majority of Germans under Hitler, 'delud[ed] themselves that not seeing was a way of not knowing, and that not knowing relieved them of their share of complicity . . .'

> But we were denied the screen of willed ignorance . . . we were not able not to see. The ocean of pain, past and present, surrounded us . . . It was useless to close one's eyes or turn one's back to it, because it was all around, in every direction, all the way to the horizon. It was not possible for us, nor did we want, to become islands; the just among us, neither more nor less numerous than in any other human group, felt remorse, shame and pain for the misdeeds that others and not they had committed, and in which they felt involved, because they sensed that what had happened around them in their presence, and in them, was irrevocable. It would never again be able to be cleansed; it would prove that man, the human species – we, in short – were potentially able to construct an infinite enormity of pain; and that pain is the only force that is created from nothing, without cost and without effort. It is enough not to see, not to listen, not to act.[76]

76. *The Drowned and the Saved*, pp. 65–6.

Such is the moral economy of bystanding. Simply by omission you contribute your share to producing an enormity of suffering. The direct responsibility, of course, will lie with others; with the authors of the misdeeds or, as the case may be as well, with those upholding and enforcing conditions of grave oppression or wretchedness. Yet there is, so Levi suggests, a responsibility on all of those who know, even the most threatened of them. Its affective correlate (amongst the just) is shame.

In some more extensive reflections whose parallel with Levi's has been noted before,[77] the German philosopher Karl Jaspers put forward a similar idea. Writing just after the war on the subject of German guilt, Jaspers proposed a fourfold schema: of, in turn, criminal, political, moral and metaphysical guilt. It is the last pair that is of particular interest in the present context, but I briefly summarize the schema as a whole.

Criminal guilt, in Jaspers' schema, relates to acts violating unequivocal laws and susceptible of objective proof, it is established through formal proceedings under the jurisdiction of a court, and it is subject to punishment as determined by the court. Political guilt arises from the fact that everyone 'is co-responsible for the way he is governed' and has therefore to bear the consequences of deeds of state; this may involve a liability for reparations following on defeat in war. Moral guilt arises because we are, as individuals, responsible for our actions, including the execution of orders. The proper forum of moral guilt is the individual's own conscience and the opinion of others, and it may lead to 'penance and renewal'.[78]

Note, however, the limit which Jaspers deems appropriate to this type of guilt. It rightly applies where there has been

77. See Des Pres, *The Survivor*, p. 43.
78. Karl Jaspers, *The Question of German Guilt*, New York 1947, pp. 31–2, 36.

inaction in face of the crimes of others, but only up to a
certain point. He writes:

> [E]ach one of us is guilty insofar as he remained inactive ...
> Impotence excuses; no moral law demands a spectacular death ...
> But passivity knows itself morally guilty of every failure, every neglect
> to act whenever possible, to shield the imperilled, to relieve wrong,
> to countervail. Impotent submission always left a margin of activity
> which, though not without risk, could still be cautiously effective ...
> Blindness for the misfortune of others, lack of imagination of the
> heart, inner indifference toward the witnessed evil – that is moral
> guilt.[79]

The thought would seem to be that if we can act to make a
difference for the better ('to relieve ... to countervail')
without definite risk to our own lives, then we ought to do
so, or else we are morally guilty. But though we should be
willing to take some risks – Jaspers does not specify how great
– we are not obliged, under this third form within his
schema, to incur a plain mortal danger. 'Morally we have a
duty to dare, not a duty to choose certain doom.'[80]

It is otherwise with the fourth form, with metaphysical
guilt. Here we are obliged absolutely. Whatever the risks, we
owe our support to people under threat:

> There exists a solidarity among men as human beings that makes
> each co-responsible for every wrong and every injustice in the world,
> especially for crimes committed in his presence or with his knowl-
> edge. If I fail to do whatever I can to prevent them, I too am guilty.
> If I was present at the murder of others without risking my life to
> prevent it, I feel guilty in a way not adequately conceivable either
> legally, politically or morally. That I live after such a thing has
> happened weighs upon me as indelible guilt.

79. Ibid., pp. 69–70.
80. Ibid., p. 71.

And Jaspers writes also:

> Metaphysical guilt is the lack of absolute solidarity with the human being as such – an indelible claim beyond morally meaningful duty. This solidarity is violated by my presence at a wrong or a crime. It is not enough that I cautiously risk my life to prevent it; if it happens, and if I was there, and if I survive where the other is killed, I know from a voice within myself: I am guilty of being still alive.[81]

The boundary here between moral and metaphysical guilt is not altogether distinct: a consequence of Jaspers' suggestion that the taking of some risk to help others in jeopardy may reasonably be expected as part of a person's moral duty, but not the taking of too great and definite a one. It is in the nature of this idea, the idea of 'cautiously' risking, that to attempt a precise quantification of what, in general, would be a reasonable risk is unlikely to be fruitful. I want, though, to comment on another area of apparent uncertainty. This comes out of Jaspers' presentation of the concept of metaphysical guilt itself – the responsibility to help whatever the risks – and it concerns how close to the individual a given crime or injustice has to be for such a responsibility to be thought applicable.

In the first of the two passages cited above, Jaspers speaks of crimes committed in a person's presence or 'with his knowledge'. In the second passage, he speaks, seemingly more restrictively, just of 'my presence at a wrong or a crime'; and he says, 'if it happens, and if I was there . . .' But I take it that by presence in this context he does indeed mean, as well as direct physical presence at a given site of crime, also something less proximate than that. I take it so not only for consistency with the first passage, but because in what immediately follows the second passage in his text, Jaspers goes on to quote from an address he gave in August

81. Ibid., pp. 32, 71.

1945, and the view he puts forward there about German guilt looks as if it should be taken in this broader way. It looks as if it is meant to refer to a sizeable public: to all who knew about the persecution of the Jews of Germany and were close enough that they could have opposed it; and not merely to those who happened to be on a particular street at a particular time. This is what Jaspers says:

> Thousands in Germany sought, or at least found death in battling the regime, most of them anonymously. We survivors did not seek it. We did not go into the streets when our Jewish friends were led away; we did not scream until we too were destroyed. We preferred to stay alive, on the feeble, if logical, ground that our death could not have helped anyone. We are guilty of being alive.[82]

One last point here. Jaspers characterizes metaphysical guilt as being 'before God'.[83] I assume, however, that there is a secular, non-theistic equivalent for it. For Jaspers himself more than once associates metaphysical guilt with the feeling of shame,[84] and in one of the passages I have quoted he writes also of knowing of it 'from a voice within myself'. But if shame and this kind of inner voice do for some people have their basis in a belief in God, neither requires it, as the moral outlook and sensibilities of large numbers of other people attest. That Primo Levi, without appealing to or drawing support from any religious faith, could write of a reaction to injustice so evidently similar to the one Jaspers describes, attests equally that there are other human impulses behind it.

Whatever the impulse behind it, whatever the basis in personal conviction or metaphysical belief, we have testimony of another sort to show that a moral sentiment similar

82. Ibid., p. 72.
83. Ibid., pp. 32, 72.
84. Ibid., pp. 33, 72.

to the one discussed by Levi and Jaspers was also felt in a positive manner, so to say, felt as a motive for acting to help others in danger. The testimony I refer to is from the 'Righteous among the Nations' as they are sometimes known, those who, often at great risk to themselves, came to the rescue of Jews in Nazi Europe. Such people may describe their motives for what they did in different ways. But a core element persists across the differences: the idea of a pressing, an unavoidable imperative to help. One Polish woman formulates it in terms of a fundamental human duty: 'What I did was everybody's duty. Saving the one whose life is in jeopardy is a simple human duty.'[85] A Dutch rescuer expresses the same thing as an obligation of justice: 'You could do nothing else ... It was obvious. When you see injustice done you do something against it.'[86] Another says simply, 'I got such satisfaction from helping out, from keeping people safe . . .'; and another, 'I had feelings in my heart that I had to help.'[87] The idea was frequently expressed in religious terms. A minister in the Dutch Reformed Church in Friesland preached to his congregation: 'By staying idle at a time when we are the last resort for innocent people condemned to die, we blaspheme against God's command- ment against killing.' The same man, it is relevant to note, also spoke of the 'tacit contract' that makes each of us his brother's keeper, a contract without which everyone is vulnerable.[88] Testimony of this kind exists in some quantity. Suffice, for our purposes, to say that the small sample of it I have given is typical, evidence of a shared moral sense amongst the rescuers that in the circumstances under con- sideration they could do no other than they did.

85. Cited in Nechama Tec, *When Light Pierced the Darkness*, Oxford 1986, p. 165.
86. Cited in Block and Drucker, *Rescuers*, p. 67.
87. Ibid., pp. 46, 226.
88. Cited in André Stein, *Quiet Heroes: True Stories of the Rescue of Jews by Christians in Nazi-occupied Holland*, Toronto 1988, pp. 93, 95.

The question I want to address now is this. How far may we take the example of these rescuers as the image, or anticipation, of an alternative possible ethical landscape? Can one envisage a moral culture so transformed as to give real practical force to the sense of responsibility for the safety of others that Levi and Jaspers discuss under the headings of shame and of moral and metaphysical guilt, and that the rescuers articulate as having compelled them? Could one feasibly entertain the vision of a global human community in which an obligation to come to the assistance of others in danger or distress was widely felt as amongst the most powerful of imperatives, moving people to action when the risks of acting were small to non-existent, making a serious demand on their consciences – on their day-to-day practical deliberations – even when the risks were greater than that, and making of shame something more than a 'metaphysical' shadow, more than a *post hoc* individual sentiment following failure to act; making of shame, and of the foretaste of it, an effective, mobilizing norm of social life?

Only by way of such a moral culture, one that would be at least *very much* informed by this sense of a generalized obligation for the security and well-being of others, could we escape the darkness of the conclusion of the contract of mutual indifference. This is a moral darkness in which it is widely treated, lived, as being acceptable that large numbers of human beings are regularly overtaken by disaster and indeed subjected to it. The familiarity of the conjunction – disaster for some comfortably lived with by others – the unexceptional character of its occurrence, no more brightens it up, morally speaking, than does the fact that slavery has been taken for granted as a mode of human coexistence brighten that up. '*Very much* informed' here may be thought to be rather too indeterminate, but it is determinate enough for the broad mapping of the terrain being undertaken. I try to make it a little more determinate in due course.

A legal and moral culture of rights and obligations largely structured around the notion that one should refrain from harming others, but that helping or not helping them is a matter of individual inclination, is plainly inadequate. It is not demanding enough given the extent of the evils that are our subject. Following the usage of Laurence Thomas in discussion of these same issues, I shall call this kind of legal and moral culture a liberal one. The characterization is narrowing, obviously. Refraining from harm does not exhaust the scope or the varieties of liberalism. I choose to take as paradigmatic a liberalism of negative duties only, duties of non-interference, where more positive duties as well, duties of active intervention and supportive material provision, can be accommodated within a liberal outlook and liberal institutional practices. But the narrowing characterization will do. It captures accurately enough what has been a prominent, and probably the dominant, moral culture for most of the duration of most of the societies known as liberal. In particular, in these societies practical indifference to the calamities and sufferings of others is taken to be a legitimate mode of personal conduct. Living side by side with them, not regarding them as one's own responsibility – to try to mitigate or to seek to end – is not widely seen as a form of moral depravity. It may be said against this that liberal cultures not only permit, they also leave space to encourage, empathy, benevolence, charity; and that it is consistent with a structure of mostly negative rights and duties to admire and praise those who go beyond what is required of them, in order to help others, as being better people. It remains, however, that this is extra to what is either demanded or expected of anyone in the general run of things, and that the threshold, correspondingly, of moral turpitude or serious wrong-doing is for its part set demandingly high: high enough that people who do nothing, or nothing much, by way of this extra are not judged to have crossed it. As Laurence Thomas writes, 'being a morally decent person would seem to be compatible with allowing others to suffer great harm'. As he also says, we do not tend to think of those who stood by to the destruction of the Jews, in the way we think of the actual perpetrators, as wicked: 'Is it not revealing ... that those who could tolerate so much evil can pass for being morally decent individuals? This consideration alone would suggest that our view of the morally decent stands in need of serious upgrading'.[89]

A liberal culture underwrites moral indifference. It makes much room for the bystander to suffering. And this is perhaps not so surprising. For the principal economic formation historically associated with liberalism, defended by liberals – whether confidently or apologetically – today as much as ever, is one in which it has been the norm for the wealth and comfort of some to be obtained through the hardship and poverty of others, and to stand right alongside these. It is a whole mode of collective existence. Not only an economy. A world, a culture, a set of everyday practices. But if it is of no concern within this ensemble, no practical, life-transforming concern, that others may dwell within reach of us in some form of wretchedness, then to all intents and purposes the judgement is that their sufferings are of little consequence. Those who *live* such a judgement upon others are perhaps not all that likely to come to the aid of people in danger or emergency. And, as I have already argued, via the contract of mutual indifference even the more minimal of liberal rights are then also nullified.

An alternative ethical landscape to this may be given various names. One of them during the last two centuries has been socialism. I do not mean that the thought of socialism *as* ethical alternative has always or necessarily been

89. Laurence Thomas, 'Liberalism and the Holocaust', in Rosenberg and Myers, *Echoes from the Holocaust*, pp. 109–10. See also Thomas's *Vessels of Evil: American Slavery and the Holocaust*, Philadelphia 1993, chapter 3.

primary to the conception of socialism amongst its adherents. I mean only that this has usually been part of the conception: embedded in it at some level, either consciously or unconsciously, an idea of mutual concern and mutual help. Some such idea is a stark moral necessity. It is a necessity against the darkness of the contract of mutual indifference. And so far as this necessity is indeed projected under the heading of socialism, the latter should not be visualized as a realm of altogether spontaneous harmony and goodness. It would have to be a moral and political order in the familiar sense. It would have to be a rule-governed, normative system, constraining its members as well as benefiting them, curbing evils amongst them as well as encouraging and generating goods, requiring duties as well as upholding and protecting rights.[90] Amongst these duties would be the duty of aid. A serious-minded view of socialism today, no less than any other meliorative conception – be it of justice or rights, moral or political progress – is dependent for its consistency and realism on the centrality of the imperative of mutual care.

Of course, this affirmation of a necessary mutuality may be expressed also in a less politically specific idiom. To cite just one example from the Holocaust literature itself, at the end of her remarkable book about Franz Stangl (commandant at Sobibor and then Treblinka) Gitta Sereny places a short reflective epilogue in which she proposes that the inner core of our being, 'the very essence of the human person', is our capacity for responsible decision. But since it is profoundly dependent on our freedom to grow, to grow within family, community, nations and 'human society as a whole', this essential human capacity, Sereny says, 'is evidence of our interdependence and of our responsibility for each other.'[91]

90. I have offered argument to this effect in my 'Socialist Hope in the Shadow of Catastrophe', reprinted here below.
91. Gitta Sereny, *Into That Darkness*, London 1991, p. 367.

THE CONTRACT OF MUTUAL INDIFFERENCE

The thought is brief and wholly general. It was also stated more famously by Kant in exemplifying the categorical imperative, stated by him explicitly as involving the obligation to render aid. Kant considers the possibility of a man proposing as a maxim for himself what is in effect a principle of mutual non-assistance ('I will not take anything from him or even envy him; but to his welfare or to his assistance in time of need I have no desire to contribute'); and he then goes on to say:

> ... although it is possible that a universal law of nature according to that maxim could exist, it is nevertheless impossible to will that such a principle should hold everywhere as a law of nature. For a will which resolved this would conflict with itself, since instances can often arise in which he would need the love and sympathy of others, and in which he would have robbed himself, by such a law of nature springing from his own will, of all hope of the aid he desires.[92]

I disagree that this is, in truth, impossible to will. One can will things that conflict with one's needs; the more especially if they are not present needs, and even recognizing the possibility that they could become one's needs. But in any case, though the thought is not expressed by either of them in overtly contractual terms, we may note the generic similarity between Sereny's and Kant's arguments here and that of the Dutch rescuer lately quoted, for whom we are all of us our brother's keepers by way of a tacit contract, or else we are all vulnerable. Kant himself in fact puts forward the same thing in contractual terms elsewhere. He does so in relation to states and not individuals, but the logic of a common vulnerability is no different. In the essay on 'Perpetual Peace' Kant speaks of the necessity 'of establish[ing] a federation of peoples in accordance with the idea of an original social

92. Immanuel Kant, *Foundations of the Metaphysics of Morals*, Indianapolis and New York 1959, p. 41.

contract'. This is 'so that states will protect one another against external aggression . . .'[93]

No matter if the idea is or is not formulated in contractual terms, the main difficulty with it, which we must now face, concerns how extensive the obligation to help others may be held to be. This question can itself be divided into two. How extensive is the obligation in a physical, or geographical, sense? How far, that is, does it reach, for any individual person, across the world's population? Second, how demanding is it, how demanding in the way of the costs to be incurred, or of the time and the risks to be taken, in meeting it? My answer to these two questions will be as follows: that, with due allowance made for considerations of practicality, the obligation is unlimited in the first, the geographical sense, and that it is limited in the second, the burdening sense, although not *that* limited relative to currently prevailing practices. In whichever sense, the obligation is in principle very extensive. I shall elaborate on these preliminary indications in the terms of a dictum which Dostoyevsky puts into the mouths of two of his characters, namely, the Elder Zosima and his brother Markel, in *The Brothers Karamazov*.

The dictum: 'each one of us is indubitably guilty in respect of all creatures and all things upon the earth . . . each for all people and for each person on this earth'; again, 'each of us is guilty before all for everyone and everything'.[94] This resembles Jaspers' metaphysical guilt except for being stated in a more absolute way. But regardless of its metaphysical significance in the mind of its author, I present it as expressing well enough the spatial scope of individual obligation in face of the suffering of others, provided that certain obvious limitations on what is possible for any single person

93. See 'Perpetual Peace: A Philosophical Sketch', in Hans Reiss, ed., *Kant: Political Writings*, Cambridge 1991, p. 165.
94. Fyodor Dostoyevsky, *The Brothers Karamazov*, London 1993, transl. D. McDuff, pp. 186, 332.

are taken into account. There will be such limitations as a result – at least – of what the particular individual knows about or can get to know about; of what he can reach, whether literally or through the agencies of others; and of what he can feasibly do or contribute, given anything or everything else he may be doing in the same sort of helping line. Still, in principle, if he does know, and he can reach, and he can act or contribute towards making a beneficial difference, there is no better reason for him to attend to the suffering of others in this place rather than that one. There is no stronger claim on him just *qua* human being – I say nothing yet of more special claims – that he should respond to this person's suffering or violation rather than to that person's. If, at any rate, our shared humanity as moral agents, or our shared vulnerability or common capacity to suffer, is sufficient to establish between us bonds of mutual obligation, it is not clear why, other than by reasons of practicality, those bonds should stop at some regional or national boundary. In this general theoretical sense our responsibility for all of humankind and our guilt for the ills befalling others are universal and unlimited.

However, it is different with respect to the amount of help any single person's duties can be thought to encompass. Here there must be a limit, or so I shall argue. No one can be guilty for everything. Nor can they even for that small fraction of the world's ills which it would entirely consume their own lives to put right. Within what is intended as a general moral code, we should not be drawn into a moral absolutism, permit ourselves a standard fit only for saints. This is for metaphysical and anthropological reasons, and it is also for reasons of straightforward humanity in the ethical sense. I take these three kinds of reasons in turn.

First, the note of unconditionality which there is in the feeling of shame or guilt at being an unprotesting (even if impotent) witness to evil, represents the demand of the moral realm against the harms of the world. By the harms of the world I mean both its brute realities, beyond all intention, and its deliberately inflicted brutalities. *As absolute*, however, the moral realm cannot be realized. That is a discourse of would-be perfection, of a moral purity uncorrupted by mundane facts, when the facts are never pure but are 'spoiled' by necessity and the shortcomings of the real. The note of unconditionality in the moral realm can only ever be at best an idea towards which to aspire and to move. For some this is the idea of God, or it is within the idea of God; for others it is a secular ideal. But that is as much as it can be: a criterion, a direction, a measure of hope. It could not just *become*, without limitation, the humanly lived world.

Second, the project of a moral culture so changed as to have spread far and wide a compelling sense of obligation for the security and well-being of others, is a tall enough order as things are without addition of the requirement for a population of perfectly moral beings, of the kind who would be capable of giving unqualified priority to their duties to others. Such a demandingly utopian ethic flies in the face of well-known facts about human weakness and the partiality of individuals towards their own interests, not to speak of any dispositions worse than that. I shall not repeat myself here, but the historical experience at the basis of this whole discussion is sufficient caution in itself against the idea of human perfectibility.[95] A perfectibility in the matter of the dutiful will is not exempt from the caution.

Third, the notion of an absolute, all-encompassing moral demand on the individual in the face of great evil or emergency, life-saving as it may be intended to be, is also life-consuming. It is life-consuming in one way where it requires of anyone that they risk death for the safety of another; and it is life-consuming in a different way where it requires of

95. See, again, my 'Socialist Hope in the Shadow of Catastrophe' below.

them that they give up everything of their time, their experience of living, the very stuff of their own personal existence, to saving or improving the lives of others. Pressed to such extremity this is itself an inhumane demand. And it is an unjust one. For to allow the individual no claim at all on her own life vis-à-vis the lives of other people amounts to saying that she must be sacrificed for them. If I may link the considerations of humanity and justice being urged here with the metaphysical one that went before: it is just an irresolvable tension within mundane reality that, to be met, certain urgent moral claims can require life-consuming sacrifices on the part of those who would go to meet them; in this manner amongst others, the unconditionally moral vies with the impure facts of life.

It may be noted, moreover, that if the wisdom of the survivors does include the strongest of counsel concerning the perilous slope of moral indifference, of standing inactively by to other people's tragedies, it includes another precept as well, with which that counsel has to be placed in some balance. Micheline Maurel, who spent two years imprisoned at Neubrandenburg, a subsidiary of the women's camp at Ravensbrück, gave one clear formulation of this precept: after some lines of Ronsard, 'May you be happy! If you only knew how much one can regret all that was left undone . . .' Or, delivered as a message from the doomed on behalf of the dead themselves:

What did we ask of the living when we were like the dead? To think of us? To pray for us? Yes, a little, in the beginning. But mainly to do all they could to send us material help, and then, when they had done all they could, oh, above all, to enjoy life to the fullest! We so often cried out to them, 'Be happy, be happy! . . .'[96]

96. Maurel, *Ravensbrück*, pp. 92, 158–9.

It is a recognition of everyone's own needs of living, even alongside the desperate call on them of the needs of others.

One can, though, set the level of an obligation to bring aid rather too low, and I want to consider this contrasting impulse by turning to the work of another who has written on the same issue. I mean Tzvetan Todorov, in his book *Facing the Extreme*. The book has much in it that is of value. It has, in particular, a salutary meditation (somewhat in the manner of Terrence Des Pres' earlier study, *The Survivor*) on the tenacity of ordinary virtue, the persistence of good 'even in the most desperate circumstances'[97] – a matter to which I shall shortly return. Todorov offers, also, pertinent reflections on the ubiquity and the dangers of moral indifference, and he points to the element of denial, of affecting not to know, that it contains. He writes:

> The misfortune of others, it seems, leaves us cold if in order to alleviate it we have to sacrifice our own comfort ... Acts of injustice take place all around us every day and we do not intervene to stop them ... We have grown used to seeing extreme poverty all around us and not thinking about it. The reasons are always the same: I didn't know, and even if I had, I couldn't have done anything about it. We, too, know about deliberate blindness and fatalism, and here totalitarianism reveals what democracy leaves in the shadows – that at the end of the path of indifference and conformity lies the concentration camp.[98]

Todorov proposes along the way an interesting, if speculative, connected hypothesis about Primo Levi's inner path towards suicide (assuming this is indeed what Levi's death was). The hypothesis is that his expectations may have been too high: thinking that after Auschwitz 'all must prefer truth to comfort and be willing to help one another' eventually

97. Tzvetan Todorov, *Facing the Extreme: Moral Life in the Concentration Camps*, New York 1996, p. 139.
98. Ibid., pp. 252–3.

led Levi to despair, because humanity had not improved but refused to learn the lesson of the catastrophe.[99] What practical conclusion, then, does Todorov himself derive from the observation about indifference and blindness just quoted?

> Must we each, in consequence, take upon ourselves all the suffering in the world, ceasing to sleep peacefully so long as there remains somewhere ... even the slightest trace of injustice? ... Of course not. Such a task is beyond human strength ... Only the saint can live in perfect truth, renouncing all comfort and consolation. We can, however, set ourselves a more modest and accessible goal: in peacetime, to care about those close to us, but in times of trouble, to find within ourselves the strength to expand this intimate circle beyond its usual limits and recognize as our own even those whose faces we do not know.[100]

The conclusion falls back behind Todorov's own argument. In peacetime: as though this were an apt description of the general condition of humankind, and not a retreat into that very haven of mental comfort which the relatively comfortable make for themselves *in* blindness, declining to see the miseries of others. In times of trouble: but Todorov says it, acts of injustice and extreme poverty are all around us. How much trouble do we need? Expansion of the intimate circle notwithstanding, these look rather too much like formulas for the world as it already is. The claims of the intimate circle are real and important enough. Yet the movement from intimacy, and to faces we do not know, still carries the ring of a certain local confinement. For there are the people as well whose faces we never encounter, but whom we have ample means of knowing *about*. As those other formulas – of Levi, Jaspers and Dostoyevsky – remind us, their claims too, in trouble, unheeded, are a cause for shame.

99. Ibid., pp. 267–71.
100. Ibid., p. 253. And cf. pp. 256–7, 295.

68   THE CONTRACT OF MUTUAL INDIFFERENCE

So where to draw this particular line? Where, between the intimate circle merely and a crushing guilt for everything?

Well, perhaps it might be, here, that 'the way down is the way up'.[101] Perhaps on the very bottom, in that humanly-contrived hell whose legacy and images press so hard against the effort to hold on today to a hope of progressive moral direction, we can find something useful on this question. Todorov himself, in a passage I can only read as being in tension with that other, more confined judgement of his, emphasizes how 'even under the most adverse circumstances imaginable, when men and women are faint with hunger, numb with cold, exhausted, beaten, and humiliated, they still go on performing simple acts of kindness', and he argues that it is up to those of us living 'peaceful lives' to recognize and confirm such acts of dignity and care as representing 'one of the supreme achievements of the human race'; he speaks of a 'code of ordinary moral values and virtues ... commensurate with our times' based upon this recognition.[102] Terrence Des Pres before him had drawn attention to the same thing: to the 'innumerable small acts of human-ness', an 'unsuppressible urge toward decency and care', even within the concentrationary universe.[103] And the two of them have not been alone; they highlight what is a recurring theme within this literature, in direct survivor testimony and the secondary, discursive literature alike.

One should not simplify or seek false and easy comforts there. The general climate in the camps was of a desperate battle for survival. It was one in which self-interest had to be fundamental and much prisoner behaviour was of an openly, sometimes brutally, egocentric kind. Primo Levi, on the very first page of his famous memoir of Auschwitz, refers to 'the doctrine I was ... to learn so hurriedly in the Lager: that

101. Des Pres, *The Survivor*, p. 21.
102. Todorov, *Facing the Extreme*, p. 291.
103. Des Pres, *The Survivor*, pp. 142, 153.

man is bound to pursue his own ends by all possible means, while he who errs but once pays dearly'.[104] But while Levi fairly summarizes in this the spirit of vigilant and remorseless struggle on their own behalf that was necessary for those imprisoned in the camps just to keep going from one day to the next, nevertheless there is an exaggeration in what he says if it is taken literally. The generality of prisoners did not pursue their ends by all possible means and nor does Levi's account show that they did. In their relations to one another they observed – even there – some moral norms and limits.

Anna Pawelczynska, a sociologist and also a former prisoner at Auschwitz, has produced a valuable study on this subject, and her overall conclusion is relevant to our present concern. According to Pawelczynska, when 'evaluated from the standpoint of the highest moral principles ... all prisoners succumbed to savagery'. Since sticking to high principle in that environment was usually fatal, there was an unavoidable adaptation of and reduction in the prisoners' values, whatever the basis of these, secular or religious. Pawelczynska gives some examples. The commandment not to steal became, for many, a rule against stealing in ways harmful to one's fellow prisoners. The ideal of equality gave way to the aspiration 'to fill the higher places in a structure of inequality [i.e. the prisoner hierarchy] with persons who would protect, not murder, their fellow man.' More generally, for prisoners fighting to keep a part of their values intact, the maxim 'Love your neighbour as yourself' turned into something like 'Do not harm your neighbour and, if at all possible, save him'. This was, says Pawelczynska, a 'basic norm', widely practised, despite the inescapable diminution in values. It is one, she adds, 'the observance of which is everywhere indispensable'.[105] The general tenor of it, as it so

104. *If This is a Man and The Truce*, p. 19.
105. Anna Pawelczynska, *Values and Violence in Auschwitz: A Sociological Analysis*, Berkeley 1979, pp. 137–44.

happens, is consistent with a remark attributed to another woman at Auschwitz, Ena Weiss; who, according to our source for the remark, did as much as anyone to help others in the camp, using her position as a doctor there to save many lives. 'Ena Weiss . . . once defined her attitude thus, in sarcastic rejection of fulsome flattery and at the same time with brutal frankness: "How did I keep alive in Auschwitz? My principle is: myself first, second and third. Then nothing. Then myself again – and then all the others." '[106]

Now, it may seem strange to invoke, of all things, this milieu, its values so radically pared down, in trying to think about the possibility of an improved, a more humane, moral landscape. However, reduced and impoverished as in so many respects it obviously was, there is a normative core in what we have before us that will withstand comparison with the fuller and more cultured ways of better times and places. For consider. First, second, third and again, oneself, and then all the others. Not to harm and, if at all possible, to save. These two principles might equally be written thus. First, second, third and again, oneself, *but* then all the others. Not to harm *but also*, if at all possible, to save.

The elements so combined, it may be said, will lead to practical contradictions, and in many circumstances they will. Fighting for his failing health, say, a person may not have energy left over for others. Or, supporting a loved one in grave trouble, he may have little or no time for anyone else. In grief, distress or other inner turmoil, you or I may not be able to find the emotional resources with which to go beyond not harming people, towards saving, or even helping, them. There is no difficulty in imagining endless variations of circumstance that will block the harmonious fulfilment of the above two precepts. Think how much easier it is for all that, and for how many people – how much easier than in

106. Ella Lingens-Reiner, as cited in Des Pres, *The Survivor*, p. 153.

the concentration and death camps of the Third Reich – to put oneself first, second and so forth, and still have something left over, a surplus, as it were, available for the needs of other people in peril, emergency or dire hardship.

More than this, in any event, cannot be expected or required. It cannot be expected or required in what is proposed for a general moral code. That is not to say that more will never be given. We know that it sometimes is, even up to the willing sacrifice of life or of a large part of a lifetime. But while more may be given, it cannot be morally demanded, and this for the same kind of reasons as we are able to call on in support of what can be demanded. I shall enumerate these reasons in the mode, once more, 'first, second, third and again, oneself'. First, if the lives to be saved through a given individual's other-regarding efforts are of worth *to* be saved, so is that individual's own life. Second, except as being at least somewhat robust, she is hampered in living her life as she would, and is of no use then, anyway, as a potential helper to other people. Third, she will have those whom she cherishes – children, parents or other members of her family, friends, lovers: her intimate circle – and no world in which the obligations to such others must be simply overridden in favour of the needs of strangers seems likely to be morally supportable, let alone attractive. Again, as the tragedy or misfortune which she seeks by her efforts to relieve will be due in part to a portion of the happiness or fulfilment denied to those whose tragedy or misfortune it is, so she herself has a claim on a portion of the same things. Each human being, in short, may legitimately give priority to the preservation of their own life and health, to their vital commitments to the people they love, and to securing some reasonable portion of what they want their life to be *for*. More cannot be expected of them than these priorities allow.

But nor should any less be, either. And this leads – not for everybody, or for everybody all the time, but for many people a lot of the time – to an extensive duty of aid and support, much more extensive a one than is commonly observed as things are. It will be hard to quantify the extent of it with any great precision. Nevertheless, I shall take it that the general idea of such a duty of aid to others, once a person's own basic needs of life and living are met, is clear enough in a rough and ready way, as are the beneficial consequences that would come from its widespread recognition and observance. There is a predictable objection that will be made here but I shall decline to meet it on its own terms. It is an objection on behalf of the selfish and the greedy, or else by those given to intellectual play in such matters, that the basic life concerns which I have just enumerated will *always* be able to be expanded to exhaust a person's time, energy and resources and leave nothing available for the crises of others, because under the rubric of happiness or fulfilment (and, *mutatis mutandis*, of commitments to loved ones) anyone will be able to put anything whatsoever they want: as many possessions and diversions, as much comfort, as costly a project or projects, as they care to name. It could be argued against this that, as stated, the concern in question was for some reasonable, not exorbitant, portion of happiness or fulfilment; a point which might then be defended under a conception of broad moral and social equality. Important as the task is, I shall not be detained by it, however. I leave this to other capable intelligences whose work it already is. I prefer for my part simply to say that, if the objection is thought to hold, then so too, with it, will the contract of mutual indifference. Either our claims upon the pursuit of fulfilment leave room, in principle, for attending to the needs of endangered others, or they do not. If they do not, other people's similar claims do not have to do so either. We are then, all of us, alone. No one is obligated to bring, and people are not entitled to expect, help in emergency. There is no obligation to those who, in Saul Bellow's words, have been marked for death. Upheld, the objection will make good a moral universe in which even genocide (to say nothing of torture, famine and all the rest) goes through.

Our duty to bring aid is, as things presently are when much aid is needed, a very demanding one. Even in the absence of great precision, it seems possible to assert with confidence that there is in the lives of many people a significant quantum of time and effort, income, wealth, not devoted to the fundamental life concerns I have outlined, but given over rather to the pursuit of less pressing conveniences and enjoyments. These are of a sort, and they are permitted an extent, that it would be hard to make a compelling case for putting before the needs of others in extremity. I mean an open, public and unashamed case, laying out clearly side by side the nature and extent of the conveniences and enjoyments on the one hand, and the extremity on the other, and affirming the acceptability of their coexistence without remedy. Yet there is a paradox with respect to the duty of aid. The paradox is that this duty is the more demanding on any given individual the less widely it is acknowledged and acted upon. In existing conditions where, for structural, ideological, psychological and other reasons, people have difficulty in bringing themselves to do as much as they might in the way of fulfilling the duty, even when they do feel a sense of their responsibility in this regard, the amount there is to be done is enormous. Under different economic, social and cultural conditions where – one has to hope it may be possible – the same responsibility was much more taken for granted, entrenched within the value system as normal and routine, seen as necessary for fending off what had come to be unthinkable (that those in grave trouble might be left without help), what there was to be done overall might be brought within more feasible limits. More being expected of everyone, and more being given by more of them, less would in practice be required of each person.

The paradox takes us back to a very old question. It may be formulated so. How, if people are not already inclined to behave in the way envisaged, can one realistically conceive a path towards the state of affairs in which they will have become inclined to behave in that way? I do not have an answer to this question; no more than anyone else does, so far as I know. It remains the problem it has always been. But there is an observation about it I want to make in concluding the present section, so as to forestall a misunderstanding that could arise from what has been the central preoccupation of this essay.

My focus on the moral logic, first, of the contract of mutual indifference, and then, as alternative to it, of the proposed idea of mandatory care, should not be taken as intended either to solve or to substitute for the problem of agency as it is sometimes called: the problem of the forces for and the ways of progressive change. This problem is as crucial as it ever was. It is a *political* one in the broadest sense: that of seeking the social constituency, the means and the strategies, that might succeed in moving us towards the alternative moral universe in view. It is the task, as well, of attempting to sketch the politics and economics, the institutional basis, of that alternative. This is, patently, a very large agenda in itself, and it is in no way made redundant by pursuing separately, as I have, the question of an alternative social ethics. On the contrary, the very idea of a humanity that would be more regularly moved to act by compassion and a lively sense of responsibility for the welfare and safety of the rest of their kind – and one can throw in the well-being of animals also, since a world in which cruelty to other species continued on anything like its present appalling scale could not be the world of such a humanity – is scarcely thinkable without the robust democratic political institutions and the egalitarian economic and social relations that would be apt to those more caring dispositions and promote them. The imperative of mutual care not only does not exhaust the agenda of progressive change, it does not even stand alone in its own function; it would need the support of an enabling, encouraging institutional environment.

At the same time, there are points to be made in the opposite direction. In the first place, those who argue – and this is more or less standard on the political left – that it is agency and politics, rather than ethics, that we must attend to in attacking the great social evils that have been under discussion here, do not themselves escape the difficulty faced by the radical moral philosopher. For if the latter has a gap to bridge between current bystander inaction and a puta-tively greater willingness to render aid in some future, happier condition, then so too does the sponsor of political agency have that gap to bridge. He has it to bridge in explaining what it is that will mobilize the prospective agents of change to become *in fact* agents of it, when they are drawn from the same human constituency as are those whom the moral philosopher has within her field of vision. The notion that 'interest', whether class or some other type of interest, will just do the trick in this domain where moral consider-ations will not, is not very convincing. On its own, self-interest, even if this is the interest of a group, offers an improbable route towards a state of things in which sympath-etic care and support for others will have come to occupy a much more prominent place. Furthermore, self- or group interest and the interest in a juster, more compassionate world are the less likely to coincide the further away are the supposed agents of change from the achievement of that world. And they *are* a long way away from it, whoever they may be thought to be. For these reasons the moral argument, though not free-standing, is also not redundant. An ethic of mutual concern and care has to inform any worthwhile politics of justice, or equality, or socialism, as much as the politics and economics of a different kind of society would be needed to underpin and envelop the widespread practice of that ethic.

In the second place, the robust political and other institutions of a democratic society, indispensable as they are, cannot supplant the pervasive activity of mutual aid I have projected as alternative to the contract of mutual indifference. The thought may be opposed to this that the democratic polity itself can do the work of the imperative of mutual care. The state, that is, might be put forward, in this context, as the institutional representative of a contract amongst the citizens by means of which they ward off their common vulnerability; as bearer of the responsibility for coming to the help of those under assault or in other serious trouble. However, it is as well to remember that states are not always reliable in these matters. They themselves err, offend, violate, break down. Even apart from the extreme horrors they can bring about or stand by to, there are the more 'elementary' miscarriages of justice they habitually accommodate. As it is, how many citizens of democratic states exert themselves over these? Unless we do, what moral basis do we have for supposing others should ever exert themselves on our behalf? Someone sits in a cell robbed of years of their life. And if, in response to this, we do nothing? Genuinely just and robust institutions would require the support of a dense network of relations of multilateral aid.

In a nutshell, although the social ethic of mutual care is indeed not self-sufficient, it has its own specific autonomy. If the politics of utopia, or of progressive change – and whether conceived as socialist or conceived otherwise – must not be collapsed into the morality of it, nor can the morality be collapsed into the politics. There is no reduction in one direction. And there is no reduction in the other direction, either.

Conceived as socialist. It used to be said that socialism was a historical necessity. It is not that. However, it stood and it stands, in its own way, for a moral necessity. That moral necessity is mutual human support and aid, the universal responsibility for the safety and well-being of others. Without this commitment we are vulnerable individually to anything that may happen or be done to us, and we sit collectively on the edge of a moral abyss. For we are, by way of the contract of mutual indifference, morally entitled to nothing at all. Today, after the unparalleled calamity of the Holocaust, political theories which do not pay the most direct regard to the primary human duty to bring aid are wanting. The more so, are any theories which deny it.

IV An Open Structure of Value

There is an unresolved and an irresolvable tension in writing
about the tragedy of the European Jews, the result of two
common but opposing impulses. One is the impulse to look
for some redemptive feature or meaning in the tragedy. The
other is to deny there could be any such feature or meaning
there. In a thoughtful collection about writing and the
Holocaust published some years ago, contributors who have
reflected long and hard about this disaster – Irving Howe,
Cynthia Ozick, Saul Friedlander – one after another
remarked upon the force of this 'urge . . . in the direction of
redemption', before going on to register their own refusal of
it.[107] Both impulses are understandable. Neither, however,
should be allowed to fill the whole of the available moral
space.

Any too easy language of hope or heroism, or persistence
of the good, risks making nothing of the brute reality of the
suffering and of the enormity of an irreplaceable, unmeasur-
able loss. Applied to the domain that we have been at work
in here, it would be an option very ready to hand to
construct, without more ado, a discourse of abstract moral
obligation or of social utopia, free from the shadow of
worldly pain. The tradition is a hallowed one. But to permit
ourselves this option would be to tell a fairy story. It would
undo the memory of the brutalities of the Shoah, as well as
of the continuous present of other brutalities, seemingly
never-ending. As I have already said once and now repeat:

---

107. Berel Lang, ed., *Writing and the Holocaust*, New York 1988, pp. 190, 198–9,
278–81, 287; the phrase quoted (from p. 278) is Ozick's.

invoke whatever moral vision you may care to, the contract of mutual indifference can just remain in place, its normativity while it prevails defying any better one. And so it does remain in place. And so it does. As people continue to be sent into chambers of horror and to their deaths, with the images of what is done to them relayed far and wide to the rest of their kind. Remembering that this still is, beware of simply edifying stuff.

And yet the other in this matter is the unilateral discourse of darkness. It is Auschwitz as the end of progress, as the end of the dreams of the Enlightenment, Auschwitz as the truth about humankind. Or it is, to cite one of the purest of instances, the American critic Lawrence Langer, who reads every testimony through a grid showing only despair, defeat and moral chaos, who flattens away every other dimension of the struggles and deaths of those who perished or survived.[108]

Let us for our part end by reading, briefly, two writers both exemplary in terms of Langer's favoured norms of judgement, writers who purvey as well as anyone or anything known to me the fragmented universe of hell which members of our species lately contrived for other members of it; and who do this without the comfort of a patterning principle of ultimate liberation or transcendence, redeeming faith or uplift, to close away the catastrophe they came through.

One of the most remarkable testimonies to be published in recent years is that of Binjamin Wilkomirski. Wilkomirski was so young when the Nazi onslaught engulfed him, sweeping off his parents and his siblings and leaving him on his own to face the terrors of the camps, that he does not have a coherently integrated and chronological story to tell about

---

108. See, below, the discussion of Langer's work in my 'Progress Without Foundations?' and, most particularly, his *Holocaust Testimonies*.

what happened to him. So he does not try to impose one. He relays those fragments he has retained – and this gives the title to his book – in a broken narrative of discrete pieces that moves between his childhood experiences in the universe of death and later memories from the time after he had been 'liberated' into a world of orphanages and foster homes.[109]

Wilkomirski's narrative spares the reader nothing. It is unsentimental and matter-of-fact. It tries to tell things as they appeared in the mind of a very young child thrust into an arbitrary and perilous domain. The effect is a desperate and draining one; for this reader as powerful a text of Holocaust testimony as there has been. Two babies dumped in a children's barrack, their fingers literally chewed down to the bone. An unbearably painful recollection of the boy – Wilkomirski – being taken to see a woman he is told is his mother, and of that mother in the moments that were allowed to them. This is not a story of triumph through adversity and there is nothing here of the sort of survival teleology or the higher, structuring meaning that Langer laments and cautions us against in other Holocaust narratives. There is, though, another scene. It does not redeem the murder or the torment – how could it? – but it reveals a different reality from within the same universe of death. Over some short period, Wilkomirski is hidden, protected, by women. He is placed by them, with some other children, in a large mound of clothing with which the women work in their barrack. It is a temporary haven for him amidst the surrounding terror. The terror does not go away. This enterprise of concealment is discovered, two of the other children are pulled out from their places under the clothing, and Wilkomirski hears what happens to them: the 'unmistak-

109. Binjamin Wilkomirski, *Fragments: Memories of a Childhood, 1939–1948*, London 1996.

able sound of breaking skulls'. He himself has to be moved to another place.[110]

And yet the fleeting image of those women, hiding, protecting. It may be little in its context, but it is there. As is also the older boy Jankl, Jankl who 'was good' and to whom, Wilkomirski says, he owes his life.[111] With other things of this kind from the literature of testimony, it stands against the unremittingly morbid pieties with which Langer's prose is so round.

Charlotte Delbo. One of the most harrowing of the witnesses to read, and also one of the most supreme. She, too, spares the reader nothing. She, too, tells what she knows in fragments, fragments of anguish and of a poetry of pain. Doomed women held in a courtyard, with no coats, bare-armed in the freezing snow – howling. Fifty strokes of a club on a man's back, recalled in the seeming eternity of their counting out.[112] Unforgettable descriptions of what it is to be seized for days on end by thirst; episodes of hope turning to futility; and, finally, the knowledge brought back by the survivor explained as being 'useless knowledge', because all but impossible to convey across the gap that separates the survivor from the inhabitants of the normal world.[113] But again, still. Delbo writes her testimony. She writes it to those same inhabitants and across the gap. 'Try to look,' she says, and repeats. 'Just try and see.'[114] And something more. Everywhere, throughout her fragmentary story, there are again women, the group of them to which she belongs, women who look out for each other, protect whenever they can, try to care for each other and, if nothing else, just

110. Ibid., pp. 46–51, 69–71, 98–105.
111. Ibid., pp. 72–6.
112. Charlotte Delbo, *Auschwitz and After*, New Haven and London 1995, pp. 49–52, 58–9.
113. Ibid., pp. 70–75, 142–5, 60–61, 224–31.
114. Ibid., pp. 84–6.

care.[115] This is not the place to explore the gender aspects of caring. Suffice to say that the image of it is more attached to women than it is to men and with good reason; and that there are, for all that, the many men who care and the many women who don't. The point, only, is this other moral reality within the landscape of evil. Once again, it does not redeem – undo, put right or make good – what happened. Yet it is there.

Cynthia Ozick, in fending off the temptation of redemptive meaning, nonetheless acknowledges 'the clean hands' of the victims and a goodness amongst the 'Righteous', the rescuers, that 'separated itself from desecration'. But both the victims and those who came to their aid, she insists, are not the Holocaust. They stand apart from it. It is the perpetrators, rather, she says, who *are* the Holocaust. Well yes, this has a certain obvious meaning; but also no. In one and the same historical landscape, there was, right alongside the evil, this other, this opposing and resisting, moral determination.[116]

There is nothing for it in the end but an open structure of value which gives *each* thing its weight. Here, consequently, the brutal and persisting weight of the contract of mutual indifference. And the hope that continues to beckon humanity of something better. And all the reasons why this is a slim, difficult, beset kind of hope. And, then again, the hope; because otherwise we 'lie down in darkness' and we live in shame.[117]

---

115. Ibid., pp. 35–40, 63, 65, 66, 79, 81, 92, 105, 141.
116. Ozick, in Lang, *Writing and the Holocaust*, p. 284.
117. The quoted phrase is from Terrence Des Pres, in ibid., p. 232.

2

Socialist Hope in the Shadow
of Catastrophe

In his last book Ralph Miliband identifies as one of a number of crucial problems socialists need to address – problems putting in question the credibility of the socialist project itself – the massive evidence we have, particularly from the present century, of atrocious human cruelty, murderous division and conflict, the seeming aptitude of our species for large-scale organized blood-letting. The sceptical question as to whether with such 'human material' a radical re-ordering of society toward cooperative harmony and altruism is not merely a utopian illusion has, Miliband suggests, to be confronted seriously. He urges us, nevertheless, against the pessimistic answer to that question, judging it 'a counsel of despair to say ... that evil on a huge scale is part of the human condition, that its conquest is impossible'.[1] In this essay, written in tribute to a life's work of unwavering socialist advocacy and consistent, level-headed clarity, I support Miliband's general standpoint, but by way of examining more closely some of the assumptions about human nature that he reviews or himself deploys in articulating it.[2]

1. The arguments reported here and in the paragraphs immediately following are from Ralph Miliband, *Socialism for a Sceptical Age*, Cambridge 1994, pp. 58–62. They are to be found also in an excerpt from the book, published as 'The Plausibility of Socialism', *New Left Review* 206 (July/August 1994), at pp. 5–8.
2. The essay first appeared in Leo Panitch, ed., *Are There Alternatives? Socialist*

The challenge posed by history, Miliband begins by saying, is to 'the fundamental optimism about human capabilities which pervades the socialist enterprise – a belief, inherited from the Enlightenment, in the infinite perfectibility of human beings'. I take this as one distinctive view of human nature and shall identify it for the time being as assumption (1). Having so expressed it, Miliband then goes on to put it, as he says, 'in more contemporary terms', as if only expressing the same thing in another way. In fact, however, he presents in the reformulation, or at least he licenses, a second, different view. For he speaks now just of 'the belief that human beings are perfectly capable of organizing themselves into cooperative, democratic, egalitarian and self-governing communities, in which all conflict would certainly not have been eliminated, but where it would become less and less frequent and acute.' I shall call this for now assumption (2), and I differentiate it from (1) on the grounds that where (1) asserts that human beings are perfectible, (2) requires no such ambitious claim. It requires only that, whatever imperfections human beings may have, these are not so great as to exclude the possibility of creating communities with the specified characteristics, communities of a socialist kind. And (2) even permits, via the reference to continuing although rarer and more moderate conflicts, the inference that there might be enduring human faults: tendencies perhaps to selfishness, to indifference toward the misfortunes of others, to undue pride or vanity, needless aggression or whatever else. Along with the run of better human qualities, such tendencies would also be, on this assumption, a permanent part of the constitution of humankind.

In any case, whether on the grounds of the more or of

Register 1996, London 1996, pp. 239–63 (where its title is incorrectly given on the cover and contents page).

the less ambitious claim, because human beings are perfectible or because the weaknesses in their nature are not so vitiating as to be bound always to defeat the collective efforts conceivable from their virtues, 'socialism's essential point of departure', Miliband says, 'is – has to be – that there is no implacable curse which dooms humankind to perpetual division and strife.' By negating this last proposition we will get, of course, the source of the original sceptical question; we will get a view of human nature according to which there *is* such an implacable curse. Let us call this, then, assumption (3). It is the assumption, as we have already seen it expressed, 'that evil on a huge scale is part of the human condition'. It is the assumption that 'humanity . . . cannot escape from the slaughterhouse, and is doomed to add, generation upon generation to the end of time, to the catalogue of collective cruelty.' It is the assumption that, as to the many smaller-scale 'individual acts of cruelty perpetrated by men and women upon each other, or upon children, or for that matter upon animals', these too 'are to be explained by traits ineradicably embedded in human nature'.

One further passage will complete the set of views I want to distinguish from one another for consideration. Miliband for his part asserts that more plausible than this last pessimistic view is the idea that:

> such acts [of cruelty] . . . are mainly produced by the insecurities, frustrations, anxieties and alienations that form an intrinsic part of class societies based on domination and exploitation. The 'injuries of class', allied to injuries of race, gender, religion and many others, readily lend themselves to pathological and morbid deformations which deeply and adversely affect human relations. This can only be effectively tackled in societies where conditions are created which foster solidarity, cooperation, security and respect, and where these values are given substance by a variety of grassroots

institutions in all areas of life. It is these conditions which socialism seeks to advance.

Now, I take the precaution of saying that, so far as Miliband's own intended meaning is concerned, his argument here, of a kind common in socialist and other radical discourses, probably does not yield a further and quite separate view of human nature. This argument is construable, in particular, as being consistent with assumption (2). For the notion we have seen to be contained in (2) that human beings are characterized by a combination of virtues and vices, or (otherwise expressed) that human nature embodies different and even opposed kinds of inner potentiality or tendency, is perfectly compatible with the idea that it is the social conditions in which people live that, loosely speaking, shape those people, bringing out some qualities, blocking or frustrating others, and so on. There are aspects of Miliband's text which indicate just such a line of thought. I shall come back to this.

I propose to wring another meaning from the passage just quoted all the same. This meaning is that the social conditions people inhabit do not merely bring out or frustrate, encourage or deform, the various qualities generally present within human beings; rather, they create them. Or, formulated differently: the social conditions, or relations or institutions, fully determine the traits borne by any given group of social agents. Human nature, in other words, is neither like this nor like that, for there is no human nature. There are just socially, culturally, historically produced specificities and differences. I call that assumption (4) and I permit myself forcibly to extract it from what Miliband says for two reasons. One is that it remains a standard position upon this general terrain of problems and so needs some consideration here. The other is that though Miliband's views do not, strictly speaking, entail it, there are nevertheless aspects of his text also – so I shall later argue – that evince a certain over-socializing or over-historicizing tendency on his part. It seems reasonable therefore as a procedure of discussion to include the limit position of this tendency for the sake of greater comprehensiveness.

I now collect up and re-order the four different views I have elicited, giving each one a brief and standardized formula.

From (3) > (a) Human nature is intrinsically evil.
From (1) > (b) Human nature is intrinsically good.
From (4) > (c) Human nature is intrinsically blank.
From (2) > (d) Human nature is intrinsically mixed.

This formulaic listing is for convenience only, and is consciously made at the cost of two over-simplifications which I at once try to undo.

The pessimistic assumption – (a) – need not require that people are by nature wholly, or even that they are all inordinately, evil. It could just take the form, and it is perhaps more likely to, that impulses towards evil are sufficiently strong and extensive in humankind that they can never be lastingly pacified, and must continue to produce horrors of one sort and another on both a small and a large scale. Equally, the optimistic assumption – (b) – that human beings are intrinsically good does not have to exclude that these beings are capable of nastiness, even nastiness of a serious kind. Indeed the derivation of assumption (b) from a formula of perfectibility implies that human beings precisely are so capable. It is just that, under (b), this capability is to be seen as less typical of, or less powerful within, the species, as adventitious and removable, as due possibly to the corrupting influence of bad circumstances or inadequate education; where the potentiality for good is more integral, more deeply laid. Both (a) and (b), in other words, can be construed in ways allowing that human nature is, as I have put it in formula (d), mixed. However, (a) and (b) take a position on the weight of, respectively, evil and good within the 'mixture', so as especially to insist on the long-range centrality of one of them. My simplified formula in each case merely accentuates the viewpoint in order to distinguish it sharply from (d), in which the balance between good and evil within humankind is left more open.

It is perhaps prudent also to point out that the view of human nature as expressed in (c), human nature as a blank, is not so much simplified in that formula as purified. By which I mean that this view is hardly ever held by anybody in pure form, but rather in conjunction with other propositions with which it is inconsistent. There is no good reason for taking it other than freed of the inconsistencies. In any event, (c) shares with (b) a belief that human evil is eradicable; but the belief is differently based in the two cases. Proponents of (b) think that evil is not intrinsic in human nature because good is; whereas proponents of (c) think that evil is not intrinsic in human nature because nothing is.

Finally (d), given what has already been said, is obviously to be entertained here in a form that makes it genuinely, and not only apparently, distinct from (a) and (b). This is to say that, with the balance between potentialities for good and potentialities for evil being taken as more open than in those formulas, neither kind of potentiality is held to bulk so large as to be overwhelming or to render the other, whether now or at any time, inconsequential or null. Base or egregious human impulses, under assumption (d), are not so all-consuming as to make pervasive and enormous evil forever inevitable, but nor are they so weak or insignificant that they might be conceived as entirely eliminable, as one day gone, as even now 'really' something else than they appear, not human impulses after all, but alienated, capitalist, class-oppressive or class-oppressed, patriarchal, corrupted ones. Conversely, benign and admirable tendencies, under assumption (d), are not so dominant as to make the possibility of serious human evil only a temporary, albeit long, historical phase which may one day pass, nor so feeble or so sparsely distributed as to make attempts to limit and counteract that baleful possibility a pointless quest. Both sorts of impulse or tendency are conceived under (d) as being permanent features of our nature, realities to be negotiated, lived with, if possible understood – and if possible tilted toward the more benign and admirable, and tilted as far that way as possible.

In completing my clarification of the four assumptions, I anticipate the argument that follows. The socialist enterprise, along with other ideas of radical human progress, generally presupposes, as Miliband says, rejecting assumption (a). I want to argue that seriously confronting even so – as he suggests we must – the sceptical question which is raised by the sponsors of assumption (a) amounts to this: that socialists henceforth should not allow themselves the easy convenience of assumption (b) or assumption (c). To adopt either of these is precisely not to take the mass of evidence to which Miliband alludes *seriously*. It is to make light of it. The hope of socialism has to be sustained on the basis of assumption (d). The goal of a much better and a more just society is to be fought for not because human beings are by nature overwhelmingly or essentially good, nor because they do not have an intrinsic nature; but because and in spite of the combination in their nature of bad impulses with good ones. Because of the bad impulses, this struggle is necessary. In spite of them, it is to be hoped, a socialist society may yet be possible.

Socialist advocacy is too often and too much informed by the kind of thinking I encapsulate in assumptions (b) and (c). Now, I repeat, the two assumptions are not the same in the way they ground an optimistic outlook: to the suggested permanence of great evil the first opposes the claim that there are deep, massively preponderant tendencies towards good inherent in humankind, whereas the second just opposes the notion of an infinite human plasticity. This difference is not immaterial. The first view has the significant advantage of being willing to deal in *some* conception of a common human nature, such as the second view for its part rejects. And I call this an advantage, because the claim that there is no human nature at all is at best a thoughtless exaggeration, one that it is impossible to uphold with any genuine lucidity of mind; which is why its advocates so freely propose or assume what they also deny, here say what they there take back, as the need of the moment may be. I have argued this case already at some length twice, once in relation to historicist and structuralist positions within Marxism, more lately in criticism of a 'post-modern' variant of the same thing. So I shall not go into it here again.[3]

I concentrate instead on what I perceive to be the shared weakness of viewpoints (b) and (c). This is their common unwillingness to accept, as significant realities in their own right with some independent explanatory weight in human affairs, dispositions in the make-up of human beings that are less than beneficent – whether of selfishness and envy, malicious glee, the enjoyment of power or advantage over others, a certain passion to exclude, cruelty, destructiveness, and a good number of other things. So far as some such dispositions may appear to leave a rather large mark on the historical record, these are always really (so the suggestion is) a product or expression of something *else*. Rendered in one conception overwhelmingly benign, and in the other entirely empty of fixed content, human nature does not

3. See my *Marx and Human Nature: Refutation of a Legend*, London 1983 (reprinted 1994), and *Solidarity in the Conversation of Humankind: The Ungroundable Liberalism of Richard Rorty*, London 1995, especially chapter 2.

autonomously contribute anything of its own to how things can go badly, the apparent human capacity for evil becoming mere epiphenomenon *par excellence*. Can this way of thinking withstand a sober look at how grim the historical record in fact is?

Let us now bring into relation with the more easily optimistic assumptions about human nature to be found in the arguments of many socialists, some views about it emerging from an experience *in* that record: of all the events of the twentieth century mentioned in the present connection by Ralph Miliband himself, the one that has perhaps done most to instil a general melancholy about future human possibilities. The Holocaust as I shall be referring to it here, some now well-known reservations about the term notwithstanding, has come to occupy a prominent place in contemporary consciousness. It has given rise to an extensive literature, coming from survivors, from historians and theologians, from most kinds of social scientist, from psychoanalysts, novelists, poets, dramatists, literary critics. But it has not left much of a mark, it has to be said, on the moral and political philosophy of socialism, and this reflects a broader state of affairs, in which the Holocaust has not figured very conspicuously amongst the concerns of moral or political philosophers in general.

It was a human catastrophe which may be thought, for all that, to pose some troubling questions for anyone committed to radical and progressive change, and it is certainly not a good reason for ignoring these questions that troubling is what they are. The words of the Polish sociologist Anna Pawelczynska, herself a former prisoner at Auschwitz, are to the point here:

People living within the orbit of European civilization today defend themselves from the naturalistic eloquence of facts which have no analogy in their experience by a failure of the imagination ... Such people, as members of that same human species to which the murderers and their victims belong, resist identifying with either murderer or victim ... [They] protect their view of the world, their optimistic philosophy of life, from the consequences of understanding the concentration camp as a dimension of the evil man can do and of the depth of contempt to which he can sink.[4]

A socialist philosophy worthy of being taken seriously cannot afford such a 'protected' optimism, shut off against the brutal realities beyond just by virtue of declining to look at them.

In 'The Visit' by Tadeusz Borowski – a survivor of Auschwitz who transmuted his experiences there into a series of unflinching, terrible stories, before later taking his own life – the narrator details some of the wretched human sights he has witnessed in the camp, and goes on:

And every one of the people who, because of eczema, phlegmon or typhoid fever, or simply because they were too emaciated, were taken to the gas chamber, begged the orderlies loading them into the crematorium trucks to remember what they saw. And to tell the truth about mankind to those who do not know it.[5]

Irene W., another survivor, speaking of how she has had over the years to attend to the needs of daily life without allowing her memories to overwhelm her and prevent her from functioning normally, reports:

Yet it's always there; it's more a view of the world, a total world-view ... of extreme pessimism, of sort of one feels ... of really knowing the truth about people, human nature, about death, of really knowing the truth in a way that other people don't know it.[6]

4. Anna Pawelczynska, *Values and Violence in Auschwitz*, Berkeley 1979, p. 4.
5. Tadeusz Borowski, *This Way for the Gas, Ladies and Gentlemen*, London 1976, p. 175.
6. Cited in Lawrence L. Langer, *Holocaust Testimonies*, New Haven 1991, p. 59.

The 'truth about mankind' and 'the truth about people, human nature' is what they call it; a truth, they both say, that others do not know. What is this truth?

There are doubtless different facets of it, but in the more theoretical literature on the Holocaust it looks, with some writers, rather like our assumption (a). Thus, according to the theologian Richard Rubenstein, 'just as depth psychology was able to expose the ineradicable dark side of human personality', so the world of the death camps has shown it to be 'an error to imagine that civilization and savage cruelty are antitheses ... Mankind never emerged out of savagery into civilization'.[7] Another theologian, Arthur Cohen – for whom the Holocaust is *tremendum*, a kind of unfathomable abyss of evil, 'orgiastic celebration of death' – has written in like vein:

> Liberalism (and in its radicalization, Marxism) may well be the fallen messianism of the Jews, the familiar secular inversion of Jewish utopian hope, but liberalism is predicated upon assumptions regarding the nature of man and his educable potentiality which the *tremendum* destroyed ... In the holocaust is a configuration of evil; it writes large what should have been recognized all along – that the oppository, destructive character of evil drains of credibility every notion of an ongoing teleology of the good that was required by the rational optimisms ... of the nineteenth century.[8]

Something similar can be expressed more indirectly, and I take as a case of this one of the few well-known contemporary political philosophers to have addressed himself, albeit briefly, to the subject of the Holocaust, namely Robert Nozick. Nozick lists the multiple and wanton barbarities, to

7. Richard L. Rubenstein, *The Cunning of History: The Holocaust and the American Future*, New York 1987, p. 92 (italics removed).
8. Arthur A. Cohen, *The Tremendum: A Theological Interpretation of the Holocaust*, New York 1993, pp. 15–21, 46–7. For an account of Cohen, see Dan Cohn-Sherbok, *Holocaust Theology*, London 1989, pp. 68–79.

read the details of which, as he puts it, 'staggers and numbs the mind'. He goes on to suggest that the Holocaust is an event 'that radically and drastically alters the situation and status of humanity'. He explains the suggestion so:

> I do not claim to understand the full significance of this, but here is one piece, I think: It now would not be a *special* tragedy if humankind ended, if the human species were destroyed in atomic warfare or the earth passed through some cloud that made it impossible for the species to continue reproducing itself ... Imagine beings from another galaxy looking at our history. It would not seem unfitting to them, I think, if that story came to an end, if the species they see with that history ended, destroying itself in nuclear warfare or otherwise failing to be able to continue.

Nozick, it is true, also qualifies his suggestion in a number of ways. He does not mean that human beings deserve this to happen; it would involve much suffering and individual loss; it would be wrong for anyone actually to bring it about. Nor does he overlook other, earlier cruelties and calamities. Perhaps it is just the case, he says, 'that the Holocaust *sealed* the situation, and made it patently clear'. He wonders, too, whether we might be able to redeem ourselves as a species, were people to begin to take the suffering of others upon themselves by suffering whenever they did. As it strikes me, however, the point here is that, despite these various qualifications, the judgement which they qualify already concludes a balance sheet between the actual past of humankind and its possible futures. If 'its loss would now be no *special* loss above and beyond the losses to the individuals involved', if humanity has forfeited 'its claim to continue', as Nozick thinks it has, and if this is so, the talk even of an effort of redemption notwithstanding, does that not amount to fixing the nature of the species by the enormities of evil in its past, to the discount of any better possible futures? More than by whatever good we might still hope to bring about, not to speak of the good already done, we are characterized by the atrocities and iniquities that have been perpetrated, in a judgement of metaphysical resignation and despair.[9]

Looking into the depths of the experience on which Nozick here reflects, it can be hard not to share something of the same mood. What Elie Wiesel has to say in a related connection is apposite. 'Examine them', he writes – with reference, this, to 'snapshots' of the Holocaust, photographs of murder in progress which we have by courtesy of the murderers themselves or of the numerous spectators to murder – 'and you will forget who you are ... Nothing will be important any more. You will have glimpsed an abyss you would rather not have uncovered. Too late.'[10] The person is perhaps unfortunate who does not know a like response to horrors of this magnitude. A mood of resignation or despair in the face of them is to be resisted, all the same, by those who can. We ought to resist the cosmic pessimism of Nozick's judgement; resist any unilateral definition of human nature in terms only or principally of its worst excesses; resist the identification we have seen made above, between the Nazi universe of death and *the* truth about humankind. So, anyway, I shall eventually get around to arguing.

We need, in resisting it, however, to respect what is *a* truth here and not just casually dismiss this as some would-be irrelevance to socialism and other utopian projects. I have in mind the sort of dismissal which is involved in claiming that an event like the Holocaust discloses nothing about the inner or natural propensities of human beings, because the behaviour patterns and personality traits it reveals to us are to be put down, either wholly or largely, to the historically determinate social and situational conditions of the event. Such a claim, it may even be thought, has a certain plausibility on

9. Robert Nozick, *The Examined Life*, New York 1989, pp. 236–42.
10. Elie Wiesel, *One Generation After*, New York 1970, p. 46.

account of the very extremity of the case. Why judge human nature, it could be asked, on the basis of conditions of life and death that were exceptional, on the basis of a hellish and in no way typical human situation?

An initial answer to this seemingly plausible question is that we are in possession of some considerable wisdom from and about that particular hell which emphasizes to us, warns us, that the actions, reactions, postures and personalities constitutive of it, exceptional and shocking in many ways as they obviously were, were also continuous with ones familiar in and to ordinary human beings in more ordinary circumstances. This was a world populated not by monsters and brutes – or not only by monsters and brutes, for in some necessary and still usable moral meaning there were more than enough of these – but by beings who were precisely human beings, with characteristics that are all too recognizable, human vices and weaknesses amongst them, common faults and frailties.

Most easily recognizable in that regard are the bystanders: those who, not directly active in the process of mass murder, did nothing to try to stop it either. These are the people who affect not to know, or who do not care to know and so do not find out; or who do know but do not care anyway, who are indifferent; or who are afraid, for themselves or for others, or who feel powerless; or who are weighed down, distracted or just occupied (as most of us) in pursuing the aims of their own lives. Such people formed the background to the tragedy of the European Jews and they continue everywhere to provide an enabling condition for other tragedies large and small, and for great but avoidable suffering. The ubiquity of the bystander surely testifies to a remarkable capacity in members of our species to live comfortably with the enormous sufferings of others.

It is not only the bystanders, however, who are recognizable here. It is also the perpetrators. The theme is a difficult one and must be treated with some care, since it comes otherwise to promote a glib and corrosive moral cynicism, actually encouraging what it purports only to observe. There is a need to understand; but without being too understanding. Yet the theme itself is inescapable. If amongst the perpetrators is to be found, as one would expect, an ample complement of sadists and thugs, there is now a large literature documenting for the more general run of them – that is, the camp personnel, the members of execution squads, the civilian users (which means users up) of slave labour, the planners and the bureaucrats and the doctors of death – that these bearers of Nazi genocide fell well within the range of psychological normality. They were not, for the most part, psychopaths. They were ordinary people.

And the same literature makes available to us a wide-ranging exploration of the mechanisms, psychological and social, by which such ordinary people could bring themselves, or be induced by others, to contribute their share to the evil. These mechanisms are many and I can only gesture towards them here: the fears and resentments focused on people who are different, and the feelings of self-enhancement or even elation at the disaster brought upon them; the thought of being authorized to act by a legitimate higher source, or the thought that this, one's own 'segment' of the overall process is only one of a very large number and not the decisive one morally speaking; the idea of its being an impersonal role, a job, and thus not due in any strong sense to the particular individual filling it; self-serving, careerist motives; a simple bending to social pressures, not wanting not to conform with the opinions of one's peers. And being implicated gradually, incrementally; accustoming oneself, as to anything in the way of a routine; for many, not being able to *see* what finally happens to the victims of the process; regarding them as insignificant morally; dehumanizing them, first in thought, then by social and symbolic practices, in the end by physically demeaning and brutalizing ones. By a combination of these means the line is crossed.[11]

It is as necessary to insist upon what is not being said here as to emphasize what is. This is not offered in that style of knowing and generally satisfied pessimism which assures us that deep down we are all so badly flawed as to become, just given the appropriate circumstances, instigators of or accomplices in any moral crime. It is not true. There are always those who refuse and those who resist. There are people who risk everything, and others who, though they cannot find the strength to do this, still do what they feel they can to oppose or mitigate the consequences of the crime in question. To explore the motivational pathways toward participation in or compliance with great iniquity is not to say that these must inevitably be taken. Nor is it to deny the reality of the choice there is, restricted or dangerous as it can sometimes be: the choice to act *against* the habits of thought and the impulses just rehearsed, upon other motives, for better reasons.

The point, therefore, is not a cynical, but it is a realist one. It is that even this (as it is sometimes said) utterly demonic of twentieth-century horrors was the work of human beings such as we are acquainted with. It was compounded of well-known sorts of prejudice, ambition, temptation, taste of power, evasion, moral failure. When they are not doing philosophy or talking theoretical politics, socialists and other

11. The theses of Hannah Arendt (*Eichmann in Jerusalem*, London 1977) and, more lately, Zygmunt Bauman (*Modernity and the Holocaust*, Cambridge 1991) are widely known. See also in this connection: Gitta Sereny, *Into That Darkness*, London 1991; Christopher R. Browning, *Ordinary Men*, New York 1993; John Sabini and Maury Silver, 'On Destroying the Innocent with a Clear Conscience', in Joel Dimsdale, ed., *Survivors, Victims, and Perpetrators*, Washington 1980, pp. 329–58 (and reprinted in their *Moralities of Everyday Life*, Oxford 1982, pp. 55–87); Herbert Kelman, 'Violence without Moral Restraint', *Journal of Social Issues* 29/4 (1973), pp. 25–61; and Henri Zukier, 'The Twisted Road to Genocide: On the Psychological Development of Evil During the Holocaust', *Social Research* 61 (1994), pp. 423–55.

radicals know as well as anyone the motivational range here, comprising, with all the admirable qualities and the excellences, also elements which are less than admirable, and indeed some of them downright repugnant. This range is simply part of the stuff of ordinary existence. It is a form of practical experience taken from every area of life: every family, circle of friends and acquaintances, every neighbourhood; every milieu, social stratum, vocation, organization. It is an experience – again, together with what is generous, loving, courageous and so on – of jealousies and vanities, petty unkindnesses and hatreds, wilful deceits, self-importance and self-promotion. It yields to us a knowledge complementary to the one we have from the Holocaust itself: a knowledge of the ordinary raw materials of great evil, those common vices and human failings which can become, in another setting or combination, suddenly exorbitant.

Lastly in this connection, there is the victim group to be considered as well. With a share of the same common vices and failings distributed unevenly across it, it too becomes stained by the crimes of the perpetrators. Another difficult theme. To write about this as it were from the outside, however carefully, runs the risk of appearing to proffer a judgement on others, of which everyone *from* the outside ought to be cautious. 'It is a judgement', as Primo Levi has put it, 'that we would like to entrust only to those who found themselves in similar circumstances, and had the possibility to test on themselves what it means to act in a state of coercion.'[12] I shall let Levi himself represent what is a rather more general message from survivors of the Nazi concentration and death camps.

In some reflections on what he has called the 'grey zone', Levi for his part firmly casts aside any levelling cynicism in this matter, writing:

12. Primo Levi, *The Drowned and the Saved*, London 1989, pp. 28–9.

I do not know, and it does not much interest me to know, whether in my depths there lurks a murderer, but I do know that I was a guiltless victim and I was not a murderer . . . and that to confuse [the murderers] with their victims is a moral disease or an aesthetic affectation or a sinister sign of complicity . . .[13]

But Levi asserts, all the same, that '[i]t is naive, absurd, and historically false to believe that an infernal system such as National Socialism was, sanctifies its victims; on the contrary it degrades them'. The grey zone is one feature of what he has in mind. He refers by this to 'the space which separates (and not only in Nazi Lagers) the victims from the persecutors'.

Only a schematic rhetoric can claim that that space is empty: it never is; it is studded with obscene or pathetic figures (sometimes they possess both qualities simultaneously), whom it is indispensable to know if we want to know the human species, if we want to know how to defend our souls when a similar test should once more loom before us, or even if we only want to understand what takes place in a big industrial factory.[14]

The grey zone, Levi says, has 'ill-defined outlines which both separate and join the two camps of masters and servants'. If it is never empty, that is because 'in the Lager and outside, there exist grey, ambiguous persons ready to compromise.'[15]

It needs to be emphasized at this juncture that Primo Levi was not well disposed towards the too facile equation of the Nazi camps with other sites of hierarchical power: 'the comparison', he has said, 'arouses revulsion in us, those of us who have been "marked", "tattooed" . . . There's no gas chamber at Fiat.' The more notable therefore is his repeated allusion, in these reflections just quoted, to the existence of

13. Ibid., pp. 32–3.
14. Ibid., pp. 25–6.
15. Ibid., pp. 27, 33.

some similar elements 'in the Lager and outside'. The Nazi camps were not for him a microcosm or the mere 'condensation' of the world beyond them; but he was willing to describe them as being 'a distorting mirror' of that world nonetheless.[16]

It is a not uncommon observation amongst the survivors. Levi again: 'the prisoner who gets ahead on the backs of his comrades exists everywhere'. Hanna Lévy-Hass (in a diary written while she was imprisoned at Belsen): 'I shall keep firmly in my mind everything that I have seen, everything that I have experienced and learnt, everything that human nature has revealed to me ... I shall judge each man according to the way he has behaved, or could have behaved, in these conditions that surround us.' Viktor Frankl: 'Is it surprising that in those depths we again found only human qualities which in their very nature were a mixture of good and evil?' 'In the concentration camps ... we watched and witnessed some of our comrades behave like swine while others behaved like saints. Man has both potentialities within himself...'[17]

On the basis of her conversations with survivors of the death camps, Gitta Sereny has spoken of the 'fatalistic lack of vehemence of those who have come to terms with the inevitability of human failings in everyone, themselves included'.[18] In the attitude she thereby identifies is joined an ancient, indeed a common sense knowledge with the wisdom brought back – and at what a cost – from the places of Nazi barbarity.

Now, a standard socialist, and more broadly progressive, riposte exists to being presented with considerations of this

16. See Ferdinando Camon, *Conversations with Primo Levi*, Marlboro (Vermont) 1989, pp. 19–20.
17. Ibid., p. 20; Hanna Lévy-Hass, *Inside Belsen*, Brighton 1982, p. 41; Viktor E. Frankl, *Man's Search for Meaning*, London 1987, pp. 87, 136.
18. Sereny, *Into That Darkness*, p. 208.

kind. It would disqualify them at a stroke from being accepted as genuine wisdom. Common sense, it is often said, is a form of ideology; and, likewise, so-called practical experience is a bounded experience only. Both are the product of particular social forms, historically specific worlds. As such, neither common sense nor practical experience can be a reliable guide to the patterns of behaviour we may expect with other social forms, in future possible worlds. Whether inside the camps or beyond them, what we have knowledge of are people who grew up in a deforming social environment. Even if it is the case that the Holocaust universe is recognizable as having been populated by ordinary human beings, these were human beings who had been moulded by capitalism, class, patriarchy and the rest, by gross inequalities and differentials in power, with the profoundly limiting and corrupting effects upon their attitudes that all that must entail. Anything vouchsafed to us, consequently, out of the experience of the Holocaust is relevant only for the type of society which gave birth to, or at least accommodated, it. It is not relevant to the prospects and character of a future society which has been radically transformed.

As much weight as is bound to be given to arguments of this general kind by those of us who entertain the possibility of progressive revolutionary change, in such blanket form they are inadequate – in face both of the terrible enormities and of the more run-of-the-mill individual failings they purport to respond to, and with which the human story is in fact so crowded. I shall now go on to offer three reasons why trying thus to 'neutralize' the negative features of this story, by just ascribing them to societal defects of a historically specific and remediable sort, is unconvincing. It is a poor basis for the hope of human progress.

First, one may bring to this domain an argument of Marxian pedigree but which ought to carry force also more widely, with anyone sceptical of grand projects of a speculative nature. This is the argument that the better society of the future is to be thought of, and fought for, as emerging out of real tendencies within the present, and not counterposed to the latter as a merely abstract ideal unanchored in existing empirical forces or in any proper grasp of them. That argument, much used (and not only by Marxists) in relation, for example, to what sort of political or economic goals are foreseeably feasible, and to the question of who are likely to be the agents for achieving them, is rather less often invoked by socialists in relation to the topic under discussion. When it comes to what kind of beings human beings are and might one day become, and more particularly to what limitations they have and how these might constrain the feasible shapes of an alternative future, it is not uncommon, then, for socialist advocacy to be couched in terms of a quite remarkable leap. This can take us from people as we know and have known them to beings wonderfully freed of the familiar human faults and vices, or saved at any rate from ever having to let these reveal their unpleasant outward effects; to people improved, in the well-known phrase, beyond recognition.

It seems, however, as appropriate to this area of reflection as to any other to hold that we have to start from where we are, therefore from the realities of human motivation, of moral weakness as much as moral strength, with which we are familiar, and not simply fly forward towards a speculative ideal. The least that one can say is that it ill befits socialists, whether of Marxist formation or of some other more or less realist cast of mind, to find easy refuge in such an insubstantial ideal.

But I want to take it further than this. For some will be tempted to minimize the weight of the point by treating it as a *merely* political one: intended, that is, to give some hope of proximate practical success, but having no deeper theoretical significance, no implication for the degree of changeability or fixedness in the human personality over the longer term.

This temptation should be resisted. The point, I will maintain, does go deeper. It comes down to the need to show a proper – some would say materialist – regard for the continuities and the resistances of human history in the framing of any emancipatory project. This history certainly encompasses continuities as well as discontinuities, some of the continuities are long ones, and some of these long continuities are long precisely because they are due to nature, both external and human (a circumstance of which Marx, incidentally, was well aware, for all the emphasis he gave in his work to historical particularity and change).

Let us take a range of common human emotions, say, anger, desire, love, fear, pride, shame, melancholy, disgust; and some familiar dispositions too, say, submissiveness and dominance – whether in a sexual context or outside it – and community, spontaneity, constancy, self-regard. Like the more basic human needs and the most common human capacities, such emotions and dispositions plainly have a general, transhistorical basis. Whatever cultural variation their forms might display, it would not be plausible to propose that they are all wholly social constructs, and the idea of some future society in which they would be no more gives meaning, well and truly, to the phrase 'beyond recognition'. This is a world virtually unimaginable by us. It is hard to say whether it would be, for the new kind of 'people' within it, a utopia, but it scarcely looks desirable from here.

Let us now take in turn – and as is not the same thing – a range of some of the less attractive human qualities and tendencies: say (in a list loosely paralleling the one just given), hatred or vengefulness, greed, covetousness and envy, overbearing attachment, moral cowardice, vanity, self-abasement, destructiveness; and then servility, love of power, cruelty; and ethnic prejudice, lawlessness, fanaticism, uncaring privilege. We should like to believe in the possibility of a world with much less of this sort of thing, much less of it, especially, that is accorded public space and the means of advancement or growth through hierarchies of great privilege, sites of tyrannical power, bouts of collective violence, and so on. But how much more plausible or imaginable is a world, even, from which these uglier human attributes have disappeared? They seem generally to bear connections of one kind and another to the common emotions and dispositions by way of which I came to them: as exaggerated or aggravated forms of those, fixations of them, deteriorations, imbalances.[19] It suggests that they too have, in some sort, a durable natural foundation, capable as they are of being brought out by a very wide variety of interpersonal circumstances and relationships – such as there is also bound always to be in any society of more or less equitably distributed freedoms. It seems more realistic to reckon that humankind will have to go on living with these less salutary human attributes in some proportion. If socialism, at any rate, will still be a society of human beings, much about them will be recognizably the same. We have nothing at present but the emptiest of speculations to tell us that the common faults and vices might disappear or all but disappear; that everything that is productive of grave mischief belongs with the discontinuities of history, with the societally generated, and nothing of it with our underlying human nature.

This brings me directly to the second of my three reasons. For there is in any case an odd feature, rarely remarked upon, of arguments of this sociologizing type which assert that nothing or very little is to be attributed to human nature. It is an assumption of, so to say, fixed explanatory

---

19. Here are the connections, with the two lists now otherwise laid out. Anger – hatred, vengefulness. Desire – greed, covetousness, envy. Love – overbearing attachment. Fear – moral cowardice. Pride – vanity. Shame – self-abasement. Melancholy, disgust – destructiveness. Submissiveness – servility. Dominance – love of power, cruelty. Community – ethnic prejudice. Spontaneity – lawlessness. Constancy – fanaticism. Self-regard – uncaring privilege.

quantity, such that the relation between (for short) sociological and naturalist explanation of human behaviour must vary inversely: if human behaviour has much to do with social conditions, it has little to do with natural traits; if very much, then very little; and so on. Or, expressed in qualitative terms, if the social is very important in explaining human behaviour, then human nature (if it is allowed that it exists at all) is very unimportant. This is not the only way of thinking about the issue, however, and it is not the most persuasive way. One might observe, instead, that whatever the explanatory weight here – and it is undeniably immense – of social structure and cultural mores, there is, as well, a weight that is due to our natural make-up and of its own considerable magnitude. There is, because as much as the particularities of society and culture may influence the forms of conduct and the run of inclinations and values within human populations, such particularities can only work, to put this baldly, on what it is *in* people to do or be. They can only work on the potentialities, and within certain limits, that are set by the nature of our species.

You can train a horse, and you can accustom a cat, to various things. But you cannot teach a horse to read or get a cat to live on vegetables, and you will not get either to be forever stationary, like an object. There are, by the same token, natural limits to what human beings can do and can sustain, and there are material needs, capacities and impulses which will find expression in one social form or another. Nothing about the rich diversity of social forms, or about the irrepressible freedom of the human will and creativity of the imagination, subtracts by so much as a single scintilla from the contribution to human affairs which is made by natural determinants of that kind.

I want to explore the relevance of this point to our subject by coming back to Ralph Miliband's reflections. There are aspects of these, I earlier said, that can be read as affirming a hope in progress on the basis of assumption (d): the assumption of a mixed human nature, with potentialities for both good and evil. I noted his formulation envisaging socialism together with some persisting, albeit very much diminished, human conflict. This formulation would allow the possibility of some continued wrong-doing also, though it does not itself necessarily entail it. In fact, Miliband writes in the same connection of a situation 'where collective and individual *misdeeds* can be turned into increasingly marginal phenomena'. And he writes, as well, of 'a context in which collective cruelty would be ... made impossible by the resistance which it would evoke'.[20] Both anticipations suggest a continuing space, as this may be put, of potential evil.

For what has been pressed back to the margins of social life still has its place *at* the margins, and presumably there-fore also its living sources; and we know well enough how the marginal can often find its way, whether creeping or irrupting, towards the centre. Likewise, a thing (collective cruelty) made impossible by the resistance 'it would evoke', sounds to have some impulses sustaining it still, to be a live capacity and not merely a historical memory of what was there once but is no longer, having been eradicated or smoothed away. I propose, in the light of these inferences, one kind of interpretation of the long passage I earlier quoted from Miliband, referring to 'conditions ... which foster solidarity, cooperation, security and respect, and where these values are given substance by a variety of grassroots institutions in all areas of life'.[21] It is an interpre-tation in which the said conditions and institutions are conceived as being, at least in part, externally blocking or obstructing, and simultaneously accommodating and facili-tating. That is to say, they put up barriers against certain

20. *Socialism for a Sceptical Age*, p. 61 (and *New Left Review* 206, p. 7). Emphasis added.
21. Ibid. – and see above.

types of human tendency or impulse, while at the same time leaving room to certain other types. Such a conception of them precisely concedes the existence of what I have just called a space of potential evil. It does so in the metaphor of blocking, which presupposes something there needing to be blocked, troublesome tendencies and impulses of a durable sort, not entirely removable by education, acculturation or whatever.

A competing conception would make the human person, or else the miscreant human person, more entirely the product of the conditions and institutions which envelop it. It is a conception of these conditions and institutions as 'possessing' the innermost core of the individual self, or as disfiguring it; so that, once given a good social environment, we would have only good individuals, without significant residue of ill-will or viciousness. Now, of course, any adequate notion of the person will need some pretty large element, as it were, of this latter kind of conception. For social structure and culture do certainly 'enter' the make-up of the person, shaping its very identity, as much as they can be thought of also as external barriers, or channels, against and along which the human-natural dispositions of individuals have to make their way. The overall balance of any viewpoint is therefore everything here. Some other aspects of Miliband's reflections than those I have focused upon so far situate him closer, I believe, to the extreme limit of this possessing or disfiguring conception of social conditions than is warranted.

One indication is his use of the metaphor of pathology. Adverting again to the long passage quoted towards the beginning of this essay, we find Miliband referring there to the 'injuries' of class, race, gender and religion – as though acts of cruelty or other misdeeds were the result of damage from without and not inner possibilities of the normal organism. Equally, his talk in the same place of 'pathological and morbid deformations' may evoke an image of diseases foreign to the healthy body, so of external provenance once more. It is true that in thus counterposing as he does explanation of cruelty in terms of the psychological byproducts of 'societies based on exploitation and domination' to explanation of it in terms of 'traits ineradicably embedded in human nature', Miliband speaks of cruelty as being produced 'mainly' by the former.[22] However – and it is the crux of the point being pursued – this is a unilateral and misleading formula. How does one adjudicate what is 'main' in this context? It might be replied that, since we can imagine other social conditions in which human beings would behave cruelly very much less than they do now or perhaps hardly at all, this suffices to validate the judgement that cruelty is principally due to adverse social conditions. But one could imagine, too, other *beings*: beings who, even in adverse conditions, would not be provoked to the amount and to the extremes of cruelty, oppression, venality, violence and so forth, of which human beings have shown themselves to be so richly capable. The point is that adverse social conditions have the effects that they do only upon a certain configuration of naturally delimited potentialities and dispositions; and, this being the case, those potentialities and dispositions merit the distinction, for their part also, of being accounted 'main'.

The issue may be further elucidated by considering another aspect of Miliband's argument. Self-consciously and explicitly, to 'the attribution of guilt to human nature' he opposes what he sees as 'the crucially significant fact that it was from above that have almost always come the initiation and the organization of mass killings'. The 'mass of "ordinary people"', he says, have seldom been responsible for the decisions producing wholesale slaughter. 'Most such collective actions have been initiated and organized by people of

22. Ibid.

power in pursuit of whatever purposes and fantasies moved them.' Miliband does at once go on to qualify any too easy optimism over this fact by adding that ordinary people have nevertheless often enough acquiesced to, cheered on or participated in the episodes of blood-letting initiated by people of power.[23] But the qualification does not go far enough. For it needs to be stated clearly also that these people of power are not from elsewhere, they are from amongst us. They are members of our species, a species in which there have ever been candidates aplenty, not just for being acquiescent and obedient to the powerful, but for occupying places of power and privilege themselves. Human beings have shown themselves very available for this and rather good at it, and it is a vain recourse to believe that it has nothing whatever to do with their intrinsic nature that they have.

A would-be Marxist (or just sociological) argument generally comes in here to say that our nature is the effect of class, power, privilege and so on, and not any of these the effect of our nature. But a different Marxism (and sociology) is possible in response. It says that human beings would not have been open, open so long and so geographically universally – and not only open, but so *very* available – to the class option of social organization and the benefits of power and privilege, if these things did not meet any impulse in their make-up. Why have they not, unanimously or in large enough numbers to be effective, simply refused the chance of enjoying huge power or advantage over others – as being intolerable to them, humanly unliveable? It is as if a single individual, having been presented over a lifetime with many opportunities to behave badly, and having taken them, betraying people, profiting unjustly at their expense, openly harming them, losing no sleep over any of it, were then to

23. Ibid., p. 60 (and *New Left Review* 206, p. 6).

plead that this reflected nothing at all about his inner character, but was the result of external circumstances only. How widely would he be believed? Even allowing for there having been other, neglected possibilities in his nature which could have produced a different kind of life, one would be unwise to let them obscure the traits of character which he had actually seen fit to give free rein.

By way of another observation on this ill-doing individual, I come now to the third reason for thinking it unconvincing to try to ascribe all bad features of the human story to the influence of defective but remediable social conditions. There is a charitable impulse that explains why we are often reluctant to see wickedness as in a person's character. We give her the benefit of her moral freedom: that she might be able, even with a record behind her of misdeeds, to prevail over whatever it was that led her to them, by making different and better choices from now on. Envisaging this possibility, we treat the ill of which we know she has been capable as being something extraneous to her actual character, in a sort of wager that she may prove it to be so. The strong desire evident in progressive political discourses and the social sciences and humanities more generally – and formalized earlier in what I designated assumptions (b) and (c) – to deny any malignity intrinsic to human nature itself might perhaps be seen, then, as a methodological generalization of this generous impulse. It represents a wager on the good character of humanity within the more favourable enveloping conditions and institutions of a future utopia.

There is no question but that this does describe something of the nature of the socialist hypothesis, taken *by and large*. Unless, in a different institutional and cultural setting, humankind in its generality can prove itself of very much better character (to speak in such terms) than it has shown itself hitherto, the hope of socialism would have to be reckoned a delusion. Taken, however, as anything more than this broad expectation of improvement, taken as the hope of a world all but free from significant human nastiness, the suggestion is self-defeating. For if it is asked in the spirit of this suggestion why people enfolded, raised, in good and supportive conditions, and leading lives as unthreatened by the more frightening or debilitating of social ills as can be envisaged, and reinforced in all their attitudes by cultures of a humane and tolerant kind, why they still might, some of them, find it in themselves to perpetrate continued mischiefs – the simple answer to this question is that they might because they can. Like the opportunity of better patterns of behaviour, the mischiefs are just a possible product of their freedom.

It is, indeed, an anomaly of one common way of thinking about a socialist future to see this future as populated by beings with a freedom enormously expanded and enhanced, and simultaneously to envisage those beings as so much the creatures of their now benign social conditions that they could not be the authors of any evil choice. They could be. It is an implication of their freedom, *ex hypothesi* greater than ever before, that they would not be exhaustively delimited by the conditions that surround them. And this is more especially the case when one considers, as I have already in passing invited readers to do, what the range and variety of interpersonal relationships must continue to be. Of mothers and fathers to children, brothers to sisters, lovers to each other and to possible or actual other lovers; of friends, neighbours, collaborators, colleagues, workmates, passing strangers and acquaintances of every degree; of carers to cared for, doctors to patients, public officers to members of the public; of the bold to the cautious, the orderly to the chaotic, the exuberant to the pensive or the weary; of those agreeing to those dissenting, 'insiders' to 'outsiders'; and then with a multitude of differences within every imaginable category – it would be an endlessly shifting picture of human contacts and situations. Within this multiplicity of forms, a freedom of putatively unprecedented scope renders the image of the socialist person as mere benign 'effect' (effect, that is, of *generally* benign circumstances) an unpersuasive one.

A shadow stretches across the vision at the heart of the socialist project. It reaches there from what may seem to be the remotest distance, from the very depths of the concentrationary universe. Socialism is often thought of as a world of almost infinite potentiality. With good reason is it, since who could now foresee or estimate the further wealth of creativity that would be opened up by extending to everyone on the planet the chances of even a moderately secure existence. If that wealth could be but glimpsed, it would astonish any person living. We touch here on an idea of unlimited human possibility. Over and again, however, those who have survived incarceration at Auschwitz and the other sites of Nazi murder and enslavement articulate something learned there in exactly such terms. 'Normal men do not know', David Rousset has written, 'that everything is possible. Even if the evidence forces their intelligence to admit it, their muscles do not believe it. The concentrationees do know . . .' Livia E. Bitton Jackson has written, similarly, of the time 'before [she] knew that there are no limits to human cruelty'. And Charlotte Delbo also: 'Did you know that suffering is limitless/that horror cannot be circumscribed'. And Primo Levi: 'I know that in the Lager, and more generally on the human stage, everything happens . . .' And Elie Wiesel: 'Evil, more than good, suggests infinity.'[24]

Can it be an accident how many who say this present it, confidently but not in accents of dogmatism, with that lack

24. David Rousset, *The Other Kingdom*, New York 1947, p. 168; Livia E. Bitton Jackson, *Elli: Coming of Age in the Holocaust*, London 1984, p. 120; Charlotte Delbo, *Auschwitz and After*, New Haven and London 1995, p. 11; Primo Levi, *The Drowned and the Saved*, p. 33; Elie Wiesel, *One Generation After*, p. 47.

of vehemence referred to by Gitta Sereny, in the mode of what is *known*? They tell in any event of a particle which the vision of socialism shares with the experience of the Holocaust. It is, to be sure, a 'small' particle only, since we compare here a hope of the best for humankind with the very worst, the most infernal product of the human spirit. But small as it is, it is highly fertile: the capacity for imagination and choice, for reaching beyond the given, whether time, circumstance or boundary. It may be a mistake to expect that great evil could not continue to threaten once there was no longer any great (social) cause of it. It could come, like acts of great goodness, like any masterpiece, from a concatenation of small causes magnified or transmuted in the medium of the imagination and the will.

* * *

It has become a common theme in discussion of the Holocaust that this tragedy now puts in serious question what have been, over the last two centuries, some cherished assumptions of Western civilization and modernity. As Henry Friedlander has written, 'Since the eighteenth century we have largely accepted the ideas of the Enlightenment, including the idea of progress ... [A] serious consideration of the Holocaust would necessitate a re-evaluation.' Or as it has been expressed more recently by another writer, 'Auschwitz decisively closed the Enlightenment era of faith in the coordinated growth of reason, moral betterment, and happiness.'[25] I conclude the present essay by agreeing that some re-evaluation in this matter is indeed called for and faith in human progress not appropriate; but by arguing that *hope* in human progress, and more particularly in the possibility of

25. Henry Friedlander, 'Postscript: Toward a Methodology of Teaching about the Holocaust', in Henry Friedlander and Sybil Milton, eds., *The Holocaust: Ideology, Bureaucracy, and Genocide*, New York 1980, p. 324; and Henri Zukier, 'The Twisted Road to Genocide', p. 424.

socialism, is tenable and necessary nevertheless, and the alternative to this hope extremely unappealing.

In so far as they were haunted by assumptions of teleology, inevitability, perfection or paradise, the notions of progress that have characterized socialist and, more generally, democratic and radical political traditions certainly need to be moderated. There is no necessity at all of steady forward movement without possibility of regression and catastrophe, and even 'modest' utopia, never mind perfection or paradise, is not only not the pre-written truth or destiny of humankind, it is not even its prevailing tendency. All it is (we have to hope) is one of its possibilities, and this forever shadowed from within by other darker possibilities. Democrats, liberals and socialists of the last century would not have anticipated the horrifying and, as it has now proved, endless killing grounds of this one. That in itself is testimony to what their shared ideas about progress lacked, the shadow of potential disaster, the threat of forms of evil which challenge the best resources of our understanding.

Neither as beckoning truth or end-point nor as linear, uninterrupted forward advance should we think about human progress today. We have to think about it simply as an enduring battle – an open process – to try to create societies from which the gravest social and political evils familiar to us have been removed; and to try to prevent, drive back or put right, as the case may be, any resurgence of these evils where or once they have been removed, any fresh emergence of unmerited inequalities and privileges, all episodes of persecution, sporadic or not so sporadic injustices, tyrannies large and small, crimes by some persons against others, hitherto unrecognized forms of wrong. We would do well to substitute for every image of progress as a course being travelled, a road, a journey, or as an unfolding, a line of development, the spirit of it being rather a struggle without end[26] – which is what it is for all practical purposes anyway.

In the light of what has gone before here, I think we would do well also to substitute a working hypothesis of, precisely, modest or minimum utopia for all visions more ambitious, whether an end to alienation, unpoliced social harmony, the elimination of serious wrong-doing, the absence of new political menaces or of old but renewable ones. By modest or minimum utopia I mean a form of society which could generally provide for its members the material and social bases of a tolerably contented existence or, as I have already put this, from which the gravest social and political evils familiar to us have been removed. The point of this substitution is not, as such, to reject more ambitious visions: universal and all-round individual development, perpetual peace, ubiquitous altruism, and so on. It is only to highlight the following: we do not need to know – and in fact we do not know – that any of these visions is a real possibility for humankind in order to know that it is a matter of crying need that certain ills, for their part all too well-known, should be finally remedied if *this* at least is possible.

We surely require no ideal of perfection, near perfection or even breathtaking excellence – and whether as an outward state of affairs or as the inner character of the human being – to recognize the need for radical institutional change. It is enough that without such change relations of injustice, sometimes terrible injustice, and conditions of life of a wretched and awful kind, are allowed to persist. Let these be attended to and the more maximalist dreams of socialist utopia may take care of themselves. Or they may not. Or they may await another day. It is of less moment. I have myself offered a speculation as to the likely creative conse-

26. Cf. Primo Levi, *The Drowned and the Saved*, p. 27 – notwithstanding the 'sociological pessimism' there registered.

quences of extending to everyone on the planet just a moderately secure existence. The case for doing this, however, is quite strong enough irrespective of what may be thought of the strength of the speculation.

I support, then, a limited notion of progress and of socialist utopia. Two other points need, briefly, to be made about this. First, limited, modest or minimal as the proposed conception is, it is not to be confused with the idea that the objectives in view are attainable through merely small modifications to the prevailing economic and social order, the order of world capitalism. The conception is modest or minimal only vis-à-vis some of those more far-reaching aspirations typically associated with notions of utopia. Vis-à-vis the world we actually inhabit, the programme of providing everyone with the material and social bases of a tolerably contented existence, of trying to get rid of the gravest social and political evils familiar to us, remains revolutionary through and through. It is incompatible with the extremes of wealth and need, the patterns of effort and reward, the structures of economic power and social powerlessness, which capitalism goes on reproducing.

It is the more necessary, perhaps, to insist on this first point in view of the second one here: which is that it follows from the argument I have put forward above about the 'mixed' potentialities in human nature that a limited socialist utopia would have to be limited as well in the specific sense of being a *liberal* political order. Opposing the idea of perfectibility or intrinsic goodness, accepting the threat of evil as a permanent human possibility, we cannot entertain any confidence in some would-be universal benevolence and harmony, or in the prospect of an end to the rule of law. On the contrary, in the light of what human beings can do and have done to one another, we have every reason to want to continue setting limits around the more harmful and menacing types of human potentiality. All the paraphernalia of the rule of law – of secure, enforceable individual rights, democratically based legislation, checks on power, independent judicial processes, the means of redressing injustice, the means of defending the polity and the community against attack, and so on – follow. The realm of freedom is restricted, then, not only on account of the unpassable boundaries of the realm of material necessity. It is restricted also on account of another, inner limitation; one that we have, by now, more than enough grounds for not taking too lightly.

Still, when all this has been said, we cannot give up on socialist utopian hope and on the hope of progress. To advise resigned acceptance of the world as it is – life-and-death inequalities, universal exploitation, widespread political oppression, festering communal hatreds, genocide, recurring war – as well as being, as Miliband says, 'a counsel of despair', is to eschew a naive, optimistic teleology, only to speak the script of another, grimmer one. It is to risk making oneself, in a certain manner, the willing voice of ugly moral forces.

Some sense of situational perspective may not come amiss here. Even in the depths, in the most notorious of the humanly-created hells of our century, there were many who did not give up hope. Plenty of others did, of course, and they cannot be blamed for it (as sometimes unfortunately they have been, in more and less roundabout ways). But many did not. It is a theme, with its own important place in the literature of the Holocaust, that I will not go into here other than to say that these many fought as they could to survive, and to preserve what they could of dignity and value in conditions of the most appalling barbarity.[27] What part do the better situated have to make themselves the sponsors of discourses of human defeat?

27. Outstanding in this connection is Terrence Des Pres, *The Survivor*, New York 1976.

If continued hope in the better possibilities of human nature can come, as it sometimes did 'down there', from an extra piece of bread, a small gratuitous act of kindness or solidarity, the recollection of a few words of poetry, then who can now say what might reasonably be hoped for if the great social and institutional causes of inequity and suffering, the great economic barriers to a more fulfilling existence for millions of people, could be levelled or lowered? To be sure, caution is today in order on the question of whether and how that objective can be achieved, as on the question of just what we could expect from its achievement in the way of the 'moral betterment' of individuals. It is every bit as much the case, however, that nobody can claim to *know*, with any degree of certainty, either that it could not be achieved, or that its effects of moral betterment would be negligible.

This cannot be known from where we stand. It is a speculation as empty as any more utopian. Although for obvious reasons not the focus of this essay, the fact is that the human record is replete also with acts of moral heroism and moral excellence, and with ordinary, unspectacular day-to-day decency. Countless human beings live their whole lives long without killing or maiming or torturing or otherwise severely harming their fellow beings. Mutual human sympathy and beneficence run both deep and wide. What the future balance might be between these better tendencies and the worse ones, in conditions putatively more encouraging to the former, cannot confidently be known. Given this, to add one's voice, whatever influence it may carry, to the chorus disparaging ideas of progress just contributes some small further weight to the many obstacles to progress, helping by a little more to ensure that it is not only not inevitable, but is, even as a possibility, more distant and more difficult.

To teach, for example, that Auschwitz gives us the truth about human nature – not merely a truth, the truth – simply serves to strengthen what truth it, unhappily, does have. At the limit the Holocaust then becomes, more than a tragic, ghastly event with its own historicity and conditions, the symbol of inexorable human *fate*, in a reversal of the very idea of progress. Humanity's accumulating crimes live on, not, and as they ought to, as a memory of the evil men and women can do, of what has to be guarded against, fought. They live on, in the minds of all those who succumb to learning this as 'the truth', in the shape of the thought that such is what we are and have to be. This is an option, it has to be said, that is not only not appealing. It is repellent. We cannot give up on utopian hope or socialism. We cannot give up on progress. They are not *less* apt in light of what we know about the bad side of human nature. They are more necessary.

For one other thing may be added finally. To accept the world as it (more or less) is, is to help to prolong a state of grave danger. This world, accommodating and countenancing too much of what ought not to be tolerated – plain, persistent injustice, stark, avoidable human suffering – is a world very receptive to present and future atrocity, a world overpopulated with bystanders. It is one in which the idea is harder and harder to resist that just anything at all may be done to people while others look on; and there be no consequence. As long as the situation lasts, it degrades the moral culture of the planet. It poisons the conscience of humankind.

3

Progress Without Foundations?

While I was writing a book on Richard Rorty published last year, I began to work also on the Holocaust.[1] One of the things that soon struck me in the literature was how little attention had been paid to this subject by political philosophers. On the face of it this is rather surprising, given how extensive the literature on the Holocaust has become and how densely populated it is by other sorts of contributors: by historians, theologians, social scientists, novelists, literary critics and so on. There is, so far as I can see, no obvious reason for the gap, for the relative silence about this vast tragedy, within contemporary Anglo-American political thought. Just to anticipate the broad theme that will be central in what follows, political philosophy has been a tradition of normative, critical, sometimes visionary thinking about social and political order. An important strand within it has been the idea of the Good Society, the dream of a just world. As such a critical tradition, political philosophy is linked by a fundamental impulse to an idea that has been very powerful in Western thought since the Enlightenment: I mean the idea of progress. But while many beyond the

1. This is the revised text of a paper given to the conference 'Richard Rorty, Politics and Postmodernism', held in London on 30 September 1995. It first appeared in *Res Publica* II/2 (1996), pp. 115–28.

discipline have come to see the Holocaust as putting a question mark against visions of human progress and so against the Enlightenment project or project of modernity, within mainstream political philosophy there is not much reflection about this, or indeed any other, putative implication of the event.

My own work at the moment involves attempting to make good the gap I perceive, there is no need here to describe how. In making good you take from where you can; you start from what you find. There is not a lot in Rorty's work about the Holocaust, there are only passing comments. Still, there are these passing comments. One of them will enable me to dwell on some of my current preoccupations whilst also referring to more general features of his thinking. This may have the advantage perhaps that I do not simply repeat the arguments of my book, although a few of them will figure in condensed form in the later stages of what I have to say. I shall begin by contrasting an observation of Rorty's with the view of another well-known American philosopher – namely Robert Nozick – on the same subject.

In a footnote to his lecture in the Oxford Amnesty series on human rights, Rorty offers the following suggestion:

> Some contemporary intellectuals, especially in France and Germany, take it as obvious that the Holocaust made it clear that the hopes for human freedom which arose in the nineteenth century are obsolete – that at the end of the twentieth century we postmodernists know that the Enlightenment project is doomed ... [But] nobody has come up with a better [project]. It does not diminish the memory of the Holocaust to say that our response to it should not be a claim to have gained a new understanding of human nature or of human history, but rather a willingness to pick ourselves up and try again.[2]

2. Richard Rorty, 'Human Rights, Rationality, and Sentimentality', in Stephen Shute and Susan Hurley, eds., *On Human Rights: The Oxford Amnesty Lectures 1993*, New York 1993, p. 246.

By contrast with this, Robert Nozick has written of the Holocaust as 'an event like the Fall in the way traditional Christianity conceived it, something that radically and drastically alters the situation and status of humanity'. With some qualifications and explanations that I shall not here go into, Nozick elaborates on the thought as follows:

> It now would not be a *special* tragedy if humankind ended, if the human species were destroyed in atomic warfare or the earth passed through some cloud that made it impossible for the species to continue reproducing itself ... its loss would now be no *special* loss above and beyond the losses to the individuals involved. Humanity has lost its claim to continue.[3]

Now I find a certain, I don't know, 'depth' in Nozick's sentiment (expressed in a powerful evocation by him of some of the detail of the historical experience he is talking about) that is missing in Rorty's observation; as reflected by the latter thinker's choice of metaphor, the simple image of a pratfall doing duty for him beside the pit of Hell. 'To pick ourselves up and try again' somehow does not quite meet the case. But Rorty's is, as I have already said, a passing comment only, therefore let this pass. I would argue also, contrary to the opinion he puts forward, that in the shadow cast by the Holocaust some further reflection about human nature is very much called for, at least by all those sponsoring a view of human nature as either inherently benign or else more or less completely alterable, to the point where all inner sources of evil could then presumably be subdued.[4] This is a company that includes Rorty himself, in his postmodern, pervasively 'culturalist' persona. In the main substance of his comment, however, in the counsel he gives

3. Robert Nozick, *The Examined Life*, New York 1989, pp. 237-8.
4. On this issue see the essay, 'Socialist Hope in the Shadow of Catastrophe', above.

against any attitude of historical resignation, Rorty's judgement is, I think, the sounder one. At any rate, I hope it is.

The difference which the two philosophers summarily present can be placed upon a spectrum of positions much debated and explored in other conversational modes, other areas of intellectual enquiry. Let me say something, first, about post-Holocaust Jewish theology. In Nozick's view can be seen, perhaps, the death of a certain idea of 'man', of 'humanity' as the foundation of progressive hope, parallel to the death of God as argued for by Richard Rubenstein.

It is an idea, the death of God, that one encounters amongst the survivors themselves. Halina Birenbaum, a woman who went through Majdanek, Auschwitz and other camps, tells how during a forced ten-day fast in one of them she vowed she would never again fast voluntarily, as on Yom Kippur, the Jewish Day of Atonement:

> Vowing this, I deliberately and with relish declared revenge on that God who had been believed in at the home of my parents, but who had deserted us all in our misery and who, here in the Nazi extermination camps, had proved to be an invention of fraudulent priests who ordered us to love and respect Him, and fear His justice![5]

Or, as Primo Levi has succinctly put it, 'There is Auschwitz, and so there cannot be God'.[6]

Rubenstein sums up his own viewpoint as follows: 'I have often stated that the idea that a God worthy of human adoration could have inflicted Auschwitz on what was allegedly his people is obscene.'[7] Rubenstein came to this con-

---

5. Halina Birenbaum, *Hope is the Last to Die*, New York 1971, pp. 227–8.
6. Ferdinando Camon, *Conversations with Primo Levi*, Marlboro (Vermont) 1989, p. 68.
7. Richard L. Rubenstein, 'Some Perspectives on Religious Faith after Auschwitz', in John K. Roth and Michael Berenbaum, eds., *Holocaust: Religious and Philosophical Implications*, New York 1989, p. 355.

clusion after a conversation which was to be a turning point for him, the occasion of a crisis of faith. His interlocutor was a German Protestant clergyman with a courageous record of opposition to Nazism, who suggested to him that the Nazi genocide must have been God's will; Hitler was an instrument 'of God's wrath in punishing his sinful people'. Rubenstein found the logic of this compelling: 'Given the Judaeo-Christian conception, so strong in Scripture, that God is the ultimate actor in the historical drama, no other theological interpretation of the death of six million Jews is tenable.'[8] But he could not then continue to uphold the idea of 'an omnipotent, beneficent God after Auschwitz':

> To see any purpose in the death camps, the traditional believer is forced to regard the most demonic, antihuman explosion in all history as a meaningful expression of God's purposes. The idea is simply too obscene for me to accept.

Rubenstein felt obliged rather to accept the 'death' of the traditional Jewish God of history.[9] He concluded that 'the Cosmos is ultimately absurd in origin and meaningless in purpose'.[10]

Rubenstein's position is opposed to that of other Jewish theologians for whom the destruction of the Jews of Europe is part precisely of a theodicy, in which the ways of God are vindicated. There are different variants of this belief. The Holocaust may be seen as representing a necessary punishment and martyrdom of the Jews for having strayed from God's law, and as a way of trying to bring them back to it. Or it may be seen as part of a wider scheme of progress –

8. Richard L. Rubenstein, *After Auschwitz: Radical Theology and Contemporary Judaism*, Indianapolis 1966, pp. 46, 65.
9. Ibid., pp. 152–3.
10. Rubenstein, 'Some Perspectives on Religious Faith after Auschwitz', p. 355.

brought about through sacrifice – a passage through holy martyrdom to a juster world for the Jews and for all human-kind.[11] Either way, the catastrophe is expressive of God's purposes, and this is exactly the type of easy redemptive move which Rubenstein finds repugnant in relation to the scale of barbarity and suffering it is supposed to redeem. He is not alone in finding it so.

In between a justifying theodicy, on the one hand, and the death of God, on the other, there is, however, a third position occupied by a number of post-Holocaust Jewish theologians. I shall take Hans Jonas as one clear representa-tive of it, though I will not be able to do justice to the detail of his argument. Once again here, something similar to the view of the theologian, reflecting after the event, is found amongst the victims of the Shoah themselves. Etty Hillesum, a Dutch Jewish woman who was to perish at Auschwitz, committed these words to the diary she kept in the period leading up to her deportation: 'God is not accountable to us for the senseless harm we cause one another. We are accountable to him!'[12] For Jonas likewise, on the terrain of history good and evil are the responsibility of our kind. In an original act of divestment or 'self-forfeiture' whose reasons we cannot fathom, the Divine (so Jonas proposes) chose to give itself over 'to the chance and risk and endless variety of becoming'. This has led by way of a long evolution, one 'carried by its own momentum', to 'the advent of man', and therewith to 'the advent of knowledge and freedom' and 'the charge of responsibility under the disjunction of good and evil'. Suffering and caring, Jonas contends, God is no longer to be thought of as omnipotent. The image of God, as he puts it, 'passes ... into man's precarious trust, to be

---

11. For a brief account and discussion of views of this sort, see Dan Cohn-Sherbok, *Holocaust Theology*, London 1989, pp. 15–42.
12. Etty Hillesum, *Etty: A Diary 1941–43*, London 1985, p. 169.

completed, saved, or spoiled by what he will do to himself and the world'.[13]

In this conception, consequently, humanity is not favoured with a pregiven destiny or end. What we possess in human freedom is only the chance, the possibility, of pursuing and securing good purposes; and what we possess in God is some 'image' of these, the intimation of a world more benign. Darkened by a knowledge of the most terrible events, this is nevertheless the theology of a certain openness: an openness to surviving hope and the possibility of progress.

Parallel differences of perspective are also to be found, I suggest, in the considerable literature there now is of Holocaust testimony and of secondary reflection on the experience of the victims of the Nazi camps. For purposes of economy, I shall focus here on some of the work of secondary reflection. There has been a tendency, understandable in the circumstances, to dwell on the way in which the experience of the concentration and death camps shattered illusions about underlying human decency and mutual sympathy: on how it did this not only through what it revealed in the behaviour of the murderers, torturers, accomplices and bystanders; but also by degrading the victims themselves, reducing them to a bare will to survive at all costs, crushing out of them every humane or other-regarding moral impulse. Such is the message that can be taken, for example, from the work of Bruno Bettelheim on this subject. Bettelheim presents us with a view of the prisoners of the camps as being incapable of self-restraint, lying pathologically, disintegrated as adult moral personalities, regressing to infantile forms of behaviour. They developed, he says, a 'childlike dependency on the guards', came to accept the

13. Hans Jonas, 'The Concept of God After Auschwitz: A Jewish Voice', in Alan Rosenberg and Gerald E. Myers, eds., *Echoes from the Holocaust: Philosophical Reflections on a Dark Time*, Philadelphia 1988, pp. 295–9.

values of their tormentors and oppressors.[14] For a long time widely influential, Bettelheim's view is regarded more sceptically today: as lacking any real inner sympathy with the situation of the camp prisoners, notwithstanding his own incarceration at Buchenwald and Dachau for a period before the beginning of the war.

This same judgement, however, of a lack of sympathy, could not in fairness be made about the currently more esteemed Lawrence Langer. Langer's embrace of the moral void comes about more subtly. Moved by a quite proper concern to caution against facile myths of heroism and transcendence on this genocidal terrain, he reminds his readers that the victims and survivors of it were faced with impossible, unspeakable, situations and choices. To read their experience through a grid of familiarly uplifting categories is to distort it, seeking comfort merely for ourselves. It is, in Langer's own words, 'introducing some affirmative values to mitigate the gloom'; or 'using language to create value where none exists'.[15]

There is a valid and important proposition here, but (like many another such) it overreaches itself. It does so exactly at the point where it urges upon us, in place of an easy but false redemptive option, the monolithic alternative of gainsaying *all* affirmative value; or, to put the same thing otherwise, where it urges upon us 'the impotence of the humanistic vision in an age of atrocity'.[16] Langer in fact has made himself the unswerving, the relentless, purveyor of unbroken dark-

14. For a brief presentation of this view, see Bruno Bettelheim, 'Individual and Mass Behaviour in Extreme Situations', in E. E. Maccoby et al., eds., *Readings in Social Psychology*, New York 1961, pp. 302, 305, 308–9. See also Bruno Bettelheim, *The Informed Heart*, London 1991, pp. 107–235.
15. Lawrence L. Langer, 'The Dilemma of Choice in the Deathcamps', in Roth and Berenbaum, *Holocaust: Religious and Philosophical Implications*, at pp. 223, 231; also in Rosenberg and Myers, *Echoes from the Holocaust*, at pp. 118, 126.
16. Lawrence L. Langer, 'The Writer and the Holocaust Experience', in Henry Friedlander and Sybil Milton, eds., *The Holocaust: Ideology, Bureaucracy and Genocide*, New York 1980, p. 310.

ness: the unbroken darkness of the experience of other people, even when these other people for their part say different, finding something in their tortured past positively to adhere or to appeal to. But with the more 'refined' appreciation, the 'superior vantage point', the 'careful' approach,[17] of the one who knows how to reinterpret what is put forth by the victims themselves, Langer flattens out the picture, gently redraws its dualities, now accentuates and now downplays, always to the one effect – to purvey the darkness. He shuts out or belittles any saving chink of light which anyone else, including the survivor witnesses themselves, may have witnessed *for* themselves and brought back with them. And the whole exercise is conducted in what is indeed the most refined, the most precious, of literary accents, producing an atmosphere of lugubrious artifice and a mournful, cultured delicacy that are false (for this reader anyway) to the stark nature of the agonies they are meant to address.

Despite all Langer's efforts to the contrary, there *is* another side to this story. From countless direct testimonies we have the evidence of something else than just moral darkness. It does not cancel or 'balance' the enormous darkness that there is. The calamity of the Shoah is irredeemable. Nevertheless, the evidence is there even in the very depths: of surviving human sympathies; of small acts of mutual help and solidarity; of attempts to preserve dignity, to uphold some values, however much reduced; of affirmations of hope and continuity with tradition, people reaching towards a different past or a better future. These traces of another – tenacious – moral universe are duly reflected by an alternative current within the literature. It is best exemplified in a brilliant and necessary book by Terrence Des Pres.[18]

17. Lawrence L. Langer, *Holocaust Testimonies: The Ruins of Memory*, New Haven and London 1991, pp. 139, 143, 146.
18. Terrence Des Pres, *The Survivor*, New York 1976. See also Anna Pawelczynska, *Values and Violence in Auschwitz*, Berkeley 1979, especially pp. 135–44.

Now I take Rorty, in his own conversational mode, that of the moral and political philosopher (when he is one), as representing the same position of a certain openness, an openness to progressive hope. His comment which I have quoted on the Holocaust already suggests as much. I go on now to elaborate the suggestion by way of a second and rather unlikely comparison: of Rorty's views with those, this time, not of another philosopher, but of the actor Marlon Brando.

In a short, incidental piece, entitled 'Love and Money', Rorty writes about a visit he made to India:

> In the course of this trip, I found myself, like most Northerners in the South, not thinking about the beggars in the hot streets once I was back in my pleasantly air-conditioned hotel. My Indian acquaint-ances – fellow-academics . . . honorary Northerners – gave the same small percentage of what they had in their pockets to the beggars as I did, and then, like me, forgot about the individual beggars when they got home. As individuals beggars were . . . unthinkable. [Rorty is referring to a passage from E. M. Forster in which the very poor are said to be 'unthinkable' – NG.][19]

In a moment I shall say something about the wider context of these remarks. But they bring to mind a sentiment expressed by Marlon Brando in the closing pages of his recent autobiography. Brando describes how, having done what he could during most of his adult life to oppose injustice, since he felt he had 'a responsibility to create a better world', he had more lately become resigned. 'I no longer feel that I have a mission to save the world. It can't be done, I've learned.' His attitude began to change one day in Calcutta. He was on the street with the Indian movie director Satyajit Ray, and 'a sea of children in tattered clothing, broken, blinded, twisted and sick, engulfed us . . .' Absent-

---

19. Richard Rorty, 'Love and Money', *Common Knowledge* 1/1 (1992), pp. 14–15.

mindedly, unconcerned, Ray gently 'swept them aside'. When asked by Brando how he could do this, he replied that there was nothing else he could do. Selling everything he owned would have only an infinitesimal effect: 'some problems are unsolvable'.[20]

There is plainly a common tendency in these two responses to a similar experience. It is a tendency to objectify human suffering and extreme want, to make them part of an objective, as it were *natural* background, emptying them of their subjective content as the lived experience of other human individuals – individuals whose inner world we can share, in conversation, sympathy or solidarity. With what Brando writes, this tendency all but reaches its limit in fatalistic resignation. Broken children become (via Satyajit Ray) an unsolvable problem. Rorty, however, having registered the same sort of sentiment – which, I observe in passing here, is a component element of the bystander mentality, rendering the suffering of others liveable for oneself by making it unthinkable[21] – steps back. He turns away.

Without being very sanguine about this, he nevertheless voices the hope that somehow, whether by way of new 'scientific possibilities', or 'liberal initiatives', or 'bureau-cratic-technological' ones, a way out may be found for the 'very poor' of the planet. Marxism, Rorty avers, was right in its thesis that 'the soul of history is economic'; it was wrong, though, in the vision of a revolutionary transformation from below. He himself thinks, instead, in terms of changes guided from the top down, by (I guess) those who can and those who care.[22] For myself I do not share this top–down perspective, but never mind. Within the limits of the occasional

20. Marlon Brando, with Robert Lindsey, *Brando: Songs My Mother Taught Me*, London 1995, pp. 461–2.
21. For one powerful representation of such a mental process see Ida Fink's story 'A Spring Morning', in her *A Scrap of Time*, London 1988, pp. 39–47.
22. 'Love and Money', pp. 13–16.

piece that this short essay of his obviously is, Rorty puts forward what is his more general moral-political viewpoint, and it is one still receptive to the possibility of progress. It is resistant to the kind of negative teleology that treats vast suffering as humanity's unavoidable fate.

I want to pose the question now of whether this viewpoint, this progressive commitment of his, has what Rorty and too many others today please to refer to pejoratively as a philosophical foundation. He says not. But I say it does have. And good for it that it does, though not that it does not recognize that it does. I shall need to quote at length here, in order to display some representative Rortian arguments. On the one hand, then:

> [Orwell] convinced us that there was a perfectly good chance that the same developments which had made human equality technically possible might make endless slavery possible. He did so by convincing us that nothing in the nature of truth, or man, or history was going to block that scenario . . .

Again:

> What our future rulers will be like will not be determined by any large necessary truths about human nature and its relation to truth and justice . . .

On the other hand:

> The view I am offering says that there is such a thing as moral progress, and that this progress is indeed in the direction of greater human solidarity. But that solidarity is not thought of as recognition of a core self, the human essence, in all human beings. Rather, it is thought of as the ability to see more and more traditional differences (of tribe, religion, race, customs, and the like) as unimportant when compared with similarities with respect to pain and humiliation.[23]

23. Richard Rorty, *Contingency, Irony, and Solidarity*, Cambridge 1989, pp. 175, 188, 192.

And again:

> This progress [the spread of the culture of human rights] consists in an increasing ability to see the similarities between ourselves and people very unlike us as outweighing the differences ... The relevant similarities are not a matter of sharing a deep true self which instantiates true humanity, but are such little, superficial, similarities as cherishing our parents and our children ... [24]

There are, I submit, two different claims conflated in these and other related passages from Rorty's work. The first claim is that human nature does not supply any telos or destiny driving (or 'pulling') historical progress. The second is that there is no tenable idea of human nature at all that could serve us as a ground of solidarity, or of support for progressive change. I agree with the first claim, but I reject the second one. And, indeed, a central thesis of my book on Rorty is that he himself is not faithful to this second claim, despite the many times he affirms it. Against the backdrop of the post-Holocaust debates which I have sketched above, I shall conclude by arguing that Rorty's philosophical position may be summed up as follows: neither the death of the very idea of a common humanity, nor a secularized theodicy with, at its core, some ideal human nature as necessary historical destiny; but rather a notion of certain shared human characteristics and vulnerabilities – in this sense, therefore, *an* idea of human nature – as the guiding principle for a viable ethic and a (merely) possible future.

Before arguing for this conclusion and indicating ways in which I am critical of Rorty's work, I shall first record an area of agreement with him by offering comment on one widely held assumption in progressive thinking. In *Contingency, Irony, and Solidarity* Rorty writes of 'the dimly felt connection between art and torture'. It is a thought, I must

24. 'Human Rights, Rationality, and Sentimentality', p. 129.

say, that I find troubling, repellent. I would prefer not to have to acknowledge, not to know about, the connection between these two orders of human experience. Rorty himself returns to the thought later in the book, in an essay on Orwell. He quotes the statement of O'Brien in *1984* that 'The object of torture is torture', and draws attention to the similarity with the idea of art being for its own sake.[25] One might also bring in Dostoyevsky here. Ivan Karamazov, in the famous conversation with his younger brother Alyosha, says the following:

> Actually, people sometimes talk about man's 'bestial' cruelty, but that is being terribly unjust and offensive to the beasts: a beast can never be as cruel as a human being, so artistically, so picturesquely cruel ... It would never enter its head to nail people to fences by their ears and leave them like that all night ... Imagine: a mother stands trembling with an infant in her arms ... They [the attackers] contrive a merry little act: they fondle the infant, laugh in order to amuse it, they succeed, the infant laughs. At that moment [one of them] points a pistol at it, four inches from its face. The baby boy laughs joyfully, stretches out his little hands to grab the pistol, and suddenly the artist pulls the trigger right in his face and smashes his little head to smithereens ...[26]

Repellent as may be, the thought is nevertheless difficult to evade: that creativity, gratuitous enjoyment in it, free exercise of the imagination, play, can be expressed in cruel as well as enriching or elevating ways. This thought bore down on me in attempting, on the basis of the experience of the Holocaust, to reconsider utopian projects – and in particular the one to which I am attached, namely the socialist project – that are conceived by many of their supporters in terms of a future end to significant human evil-

25. *Contingency, Irony, and Solidarity*, pp. 146, 180.
26. Fyodor Dostoyevsky, *The Brothers Karamazov*, London 1993, transl. D. McDuff, p. 274. The final ellipsis is in the original.

doing. One standard feature of this sort of thinking has been the vision of a very expansive sphere of human freedom, of a sphere of nearly unlimited creative possibility.

A shadow, however, is thrown across every such vision by the central depravity of our century. Listen to how some of the survivors of it speak. David Rousset: 'Normal men do not know that everything is possible. Even if the evidence forces their intelligence to admit it, their muscles do not believe it. The concentrationees do know...' Livia E. Bitton Jackson: 'It was before I knew that there are no limits to human cruelty'. Charlotte Delbo: 'Did you know that suffering is limitless/that horror cannot be circumscribed'. Primo Levi: 'I know that in the Lager, and more generally on the human stage, everything happens...' Elie Wiesel: 'Evil, more than good, suggests infinity.'[27]

If human freedom and an endlessly inventive imagination can generate great evil as well as great beauty, collective enjoyment, great good, most utopians – socialists prominent amongst these – tend to eliminate the problem by envisaging more or less benign future social conditions as the cradle and nursery of changed future people. But is there not a contradiction here: between the notion of human beings acting at last in *freedom*, and the notion of these same human beings as all but the creatures of their now benign social conditions, effectively just conditioned by them? A feasible conception of progress today needs to come to terms with the likely persistence of some of the less pleasant tendencies and potentialities that are lodged within the characteristic make-up of human beings.[28]

27. David Rousset, *The Other Kingdom*, New York 1947, p. 168; Livia E. Bitton Jackson, *Elli: Coming of Age in the Holocaust*, London 1984, p. 120; Charlotte Delbo, *Auschwitz and After*, New Haven and London 1995, p. 11; Primo Levi, *The Drowned and the Saved*, London 1989, p. 33; Elie Wiesel, *One Generation After*, New York 1970, p. 47.
28. For a more extensive discussion of these issues, see 'Socialist Hope in the Shadow of Catastrophe' above.

Now, Rorty for his part offers a notion of moral progress as being in the direction of greater human solidarity. How does he commend this to us? Not, so he claims, on the basis of appealing to any human universal, since identification with humanity as such is, he says, impossible.[29] He commends it rather via a sense of moral community: as one might have, for example, with one's fellow nationals or co-religionists, and which one can then try to extend to more and more people by progressively expanding the notion of 'one of us'.[30] Moral sentiment in this is more important than moral rationality or principle.[31] And, as one amongst other kinds of universal, the very notion of a common human nature is to be renounced.

In my book I identify three meanings of the concept of human nature to which Rorty's denials purport to apply: human nature as a set of shared, transhistorical character-istics; human nature as a set of shared, transhistorical *and* species-specific characteristics; and human nature as a set of either one sort or the other which serves us as a moral reference point. I show that he relies, in spite of his own repeated denials, on a concept of human nature in all of these three meanings.[32] Here I will limit myself simply to this very condensed explanation: a commitment to progress in Rorty's sense, the sense of a greater (and greater) human solidarity, cannot do without the kind of universalist under-pinning he himself wishes to renounce – and nor does he do without it.

Thus, the simplest thing to say about the suggestion that we should start from our fellow Americans – or whoever – and work outwards from there by expanding the notion of

29. *Contingency, Irony, and Solidarity*, p. 198.
30. Ibid., pp. 189–98.
31. 'Human Rights, Rationality, and Sentimentality', pp. 112–34.
32. Norman Geras, *Solidarity in the Conversation of Humankind: The Ungroundable Liberalism of Richard Rorty*, London 1995, pp. 47–70.

'one of us', is that the suggestion will either work, and thereby it will undo Rorty's own premisses, or else it will *not* work. One can move from fellow Americans, for instance, to Mexicans, Brazilians and then others, or from fellow Catholics to all Christians, and then to Muslims and Jews. But either this process stops short somewhere, so as to leave a 'one of them' that can be contrasted with the 'one of us'; and then Africans, say, or atheists, are excluded from the sense of moral community, and they can go hungry or be massacred for all one cares. This is a strange kind of 'human' solidarity. Or, on the other hand, the process need not stop short, and one's sense of moral community can be extended to all human beings. In this case the identification with humanity as such is not impossible after all. Why should it be? Why, for someone who allows that a sense of 'we' might cover all fellow Americans, and then be expanded? Americans are some 250 million people. With only Mexicans and Brazilians added on, 'we' comes to embrace approximately 500 million people. If this scale of identification is feasible, then so is humanity in general. It is not credible that the relevant limit to human compassion lies somewhere beyond several hundred million people.[33]

The fact is that there are other modes of identification than communitarian ones, and Rorty himself knows what they are. They are the very similarities in light of which he says particularist differences can come to be seen as unimportant. They are things like pain and humiliation, cherishing one's loved ones and grieving for them, and then poetry and yet other things besides. In appealing to such similarities, Rorty appeals to nothing other than the idea of a common humanity.

For much of the time and for millions of people the world

---

33. This paragraph summarizes *Solidarity in the Conversation of Humankind*, pp. 76–8.

has been a harsh, sometimes a terrible, place. 'Nobody has come up with a better project' than that of trying to make a world that would be fit for all human beings. It is to Richard Rorty's credit that he remains attached to this project, some misguided philosophical commitments notwithstanding.

Marxists before the Holocaust

I shall begin here from an astonishing fact. In December 1938, in an appeal to American Jews, Leon Trotsky in a certain manner predicted the impending Jewish catastrophe. Here is what he wrote:

> It is possible to imagine without difficulty what awaits the Jews at the mere outbreak of the future world war. But even without war the next development of world reaction signifies with certainty the *physical extermination of the Jews*.[1]

This was just a few weeks after Kristallnacht and it was one month before Hitler's famous Reichstag speech of 30 January 1939 in which he 'prophesied' the annihilation of European Jewry in the event of a world war.

I call Trotsky's prediction an astonishing fact. For it is a common and well-grounded theme in the literature of the Holocaust that the disaster was not really predictable. It was outside the range of normal experience and of sober political projection or indeed imagination. Even once the tragedy began to unfold, many people found the information on what was being done to the Jews hard to absorb, hard to connect

1. Leon Trotsky, *On the Jewish Question*, New York 1970, p. 29, emphasis in the original.

up into a unified picture of comprehensive genocide, hard to believe; and this applied to wide sections of the Jewish population itself. Then, after the event, its enormity has seemed to many difficult to grasp. It has seemed to be in some measure beyond understanding and explanation. We have the evidence of such a reaction from none other than Trotsky's great biographer. Referring to 'the absolute uniqueness of the catastrophe', Isaac Deutscher would later write:

> The fury of Nazism, which was bent on the unconditional extermination of every Jewish man, woman, and child within its reach, passes the comprehension of a historian, who tries to uncover the motives of human behaviour and to discern the interests behind the motives. Who can analyse the motives and the interests behind the enormities of Auschwitz? ... [W]e are confronted here by a huge and ominous mystery of the degeneration of the human character that will forever baffle and terrify mankind.[2]

2. Isaac Deutscher, 'The Jewish Tragedy and the Historian', in his *The Non-Jewish Jew and other essays*, London 1968, pp. 163–4. For discussion of the unpredictability of the Holocaust and the initial difficulties of belief, see: Yehuda Bauer, *The Holocaust in Historical Perspective*, Seattle 1978, pp. 7, 16–22, 81; Jacob Katz, 'Was the Holocaust Predictable?', in Y. Bauer and N. Rotenstreich, eds., *The Holocaust as Historical Experience*, New York 1981, pp. 23–41; Walter Laqueur, *The Terrible Secret*, London 1980, pp. 1–10; and Michael Marrus, *The Holocaust in History*, London 1987, pp. 156–64. Yehuda Bauer goes so far as to say that nobody predicted the Holocaust, whatever may have been claimed to the contrary; that the most that anyone could have envisaged was 'pogroms, economic destruction, hunger, or forced emigration', not 'the mass murder of millions of human beings'. I have no way of knowing whether Bauer is familiar with Trotsky's quoted remarks but, however things may be in general on this score, I do not see how those remarks can be taken in the way Bauer suggests. It is not only that Trotsky puts it so, and emphasizes: the *physical extermination* of the Jews; repeating the point, indeed, a few lines on with the claim that 'not only their political but also their physical fate' is tied to the struggle of the international proletariat. It is also that immediately before making this prediction he speaks of an ever-diminishing space for the Jews on the planet, with the number of countries that expel them ceaselessly growing, the number willing to accept them always decreasing. In *this* context 'physical extermination of the Jews' is what he sees as logically coming next and what he actually says; and physical extermination of the Jews is what Hitler and his accomplices undertook. Naturally, this is not to say that Trotsky foresaw the specific form of what was to happen.

How are we to account for Trotsky's prescience in this matter? Was it perhaps just some sort of stray, dark intuition? Or was it rather a hypothesis founded on the forms of knowledge which he brought to trying to understand the realities of his time? I shall in due course propose as an answer that it was something in between. But I will come to this answer by way of a critical review of Ernest Mandel's thinking on the same subject. This is the main purpose of what I want to present here, though my aim will be as well, through it, to offer some more general reflections on Marxism as a body of theory in relation to the Nazi genocide against the Jews.

I say a critical review of Mandel's thinking on the subject and critical is what it will be; although it will be somewhat less so in relation to his later views as compared with the earlier ones, since there was an internal development and enlargement of these. Still, overall, it will be critical. And I am bound to observe, therefore, that so critical a review may seem out of place on the occasion, devoted as it is to registering and honouring Mandel's achievement.[3] Let me just say three things about this. First, like other participants here I held, and I hold, Mandel's life's work in the highest regard, and nothing in what follows affects that. Second, in the proper place I have recorded my own debts to him. In particular, his work helped me to an understanding of something centrally important in the thinking of Rosa Luxemburg, as also in any rounded conception of emancipatory socialist struggle.[4] (I refer by this not only to what he wrote specifically about Rosa Luxemburg but also to his political

3. This is the revised text of a paper presented to the conference 'The Contribution of Ernest Mandel to Marxist Theory', held in Amsterdam, 4–6 July 1996. It will be part of a volume of essays about Mandel's work arising from that conference, and has appeared also in *New Left Review* 224 (July/August 1997).

4. See my *The Legacy of Rosa Luxemburg*, London 1976, p. 119.

writings more generally.) Third, Mandel himself, I believe, would not have been happy with anything less: anything less than the frankest appraisal on whatever question, and if frankly critical, then so be it.

An early effort by him to take the measure of the Jewish tragedy is an article of 1946, 'La question juive au lendemain de la deuxième guerre mondiale'. Please keep in mind that it was written by Mandel at the age of 22 or 23, and also (in light of that date, 1946) how much difficulty in general people have had, over several decades, in facing up to the implications of this catastrophe. Mandel begins by evoking the horrors of it, and he then gestures towards the sort of uncomprehending response I have already illustrated with the words of Isaac Deutscher. The human imagination has trouble grasping the significance of the experience, Mandel writes; the misfortune of the Jews seems 'absurd'. The mind 'refuses to admit that material interests could have determined, in cold logic, the extermination of these innumerable defenceless beings'.[5]

This is not, however, the response that Mandel for his part wants to recommend. The fate of the European Jews he firmly situates, as being explicable by it, in the broader context of the mortal crisis of capitalism; and in the context, a product of this crisis, of the other horrors of the Second World War. It is 'capitalism [that is] responsible for their [the Jews'] tragic fate and for the impasse in which the whole of humanity finds itself'.[6] The Nazi genocide against the Jews is also 'contextualized' by the young Mandel by reference to certain actions and attitudes of the Allied powers: the deportation of ethnic Germans from parts of east and central Europe at the end of the war; the callousness of the British

5. E. Germain [Mandel], 'La question juive au lendemain de la deuxième guerre mondiale', afterword to A. Léon, Conception matérialiste de la question juive, Paris 1946, p. I.
6. Ibid., p. VI.

towards mass suffering in India, or of the Americans in connection with the use of the atomic bomb at Hiroshima; the responsibility borne by the whole capitalist order, by 'all the governments of the world', in not coming to the aid of the Jewish people. And next to 5 million murdered Jews (the figure Mandel gives), 'one finds the 60 million victims of the imperialist war'. The general spirit of this assessment is captured by formulations like the following:

> The barbarous treatment of the Jews by Hitlerite imperialism has only pushed to paroxysm the barbarism of the habitual methods of imperialism in our epoch.

> Far from being isolated from, or opposed to, the destiny of humanity, the Jewish tragedy only announces to other peoples their future fate if the decline of capitalism continues at its present rate.[7]

This early attempt by Mandel to assess the significance of the Shoah is marked, in my opinion, by a triple weakness. It can be described in terms of the three polar oppositions set out below. The destruction of the Jews of Europe:

is comparable to other crimes / is singular or unique;
is rationally explicable / is beyond comprehension;
is the product of capitalism and imperialism / is due to some other combination of factors.

Now, I do not believe any adequate assessment can be made by just embracing either one pole or the other of these three oppositions. A certain (particular) intermediate standpoint is called for in relation to each. The weakness of this initial article by Mandel is that he pretty well does embrace the first pole of each opposition. According to him, the destruction of the Jews of Europe is *rationally explicable* as the *product of*

7. Ibid., pp. I–III.

imperialist capitalism, and as such it is manifestly *comparable* to the other barbarisms which this socio-economic formation throws up. That both the specificity of the event and a certain 'elusiveness', such as very many people have felt and expressed about it, are thereby levelled or lost, is perhaps best brought out by this hypothesis towards the end of the essay:

> [I]t is not just possible but probable that an American fascist movement will go beyond, in its technical 'perfection', the brutalities of Nazi anti-semitism. If the next decade is not witness to the proletarian revolution in the United States, it will prepare for American Jewry hecatombs that will surpass Auschwitz and Maidanek in horror.[8]

The Holocaust is here turned into a more or less regular type of occurrence of our epoch. Terrible as it may have been, it only anticipates much worse, and this within a decade or two should capitalism survive.

I may as well indicate before proceeding any further that I do not think Ernest Mandel ever made good the three weaknesses I have identified from this early article (and will shortly come back to enlarge upon). Although in the last decade of his life, returning to the same subject, he would elaborate a view of it more qualified and enriched, the same weaknesses in one way or another were to remain.

That they continued at least into the 1960s and 1970s can be marked by drawing attention to a certain absence. In his Introduction of 1969 to the collection of Trotsky's texts *The Struggle Against Fascism in Germany*, Mandel does not even directly mention the Holocaust. The same thing in the relevant chapter (chapter 8) of his *Trotsky*, published in 1979. There are some generic references to 'an advancing barbarism', and to threats to the survival of 'broad human

8. Ibid., p. XI.

groups' or to 'human civilization' itself. But this is as close as he gets.[9] To be sure, the writings of Trotsky that Mandel here introduces themselves predate the 'Final Solution', so one would not expect the topic to loom enormously large in what he says about them. Even so, Trotsky *before* the event, in some well-known passages to which I shall later return, seems to anticipate the extremes of barbarism that a triumphant National Socialism would portend. Is it not remarkable that twenty-five, and thirty-five, years *after* the event, in full awareness of what one of these extremes turned out to be, Mandel finds no place to mention it directly, much less to discuss it, in presenting Trotsky's ideas about the rise and the victory of Nazism?

What he does present is a general theory of *fascism*: a theory of it centred on the crushing of the workers' movement, and articulated through Marxist concepts of class, capitalist economic crisis, the different political forms and methods of rule of the capitalist state.[10] We may note two particular claims made by Mandel in presenting this theory. First, fascism, he insists, is 'a universal phenomenon that knows no geographical boundaries [and which] struck roots in *all* imperialist lands'; 'attempts at explanation that chiefly emphasize this or that national peculiarity are wholly inadequate'.[11] While I have, on one level, no quarrel with this, it is nevertheless an optic likely to discourage attention towards a certain specificity of German National Socialism and of one of its policies. Second, the superiority of the Marxist method of social analysis, Mandel contends, lies in its total character. It seeks 'to comprehend all aspects of social

9. See the Introduction to Leon Trotsky, *The Struggle Against Fascism in Germany*, New York 1971, pp. 9, 39; and Ernest Mandel, *Trotsky: A Study in the Dynamic of his Thought*, London 1979, p. 88.
10. In this connection, see particularly *The Struggle Against Fascism in Germany*, pp. 17–21.
11. Ibid., p. 15.

activity as connected with and structurally coordinated to one another.' This is a thesis put forward also at other places in his writings. But it is not tested here against the difficulties of explaining the 'Final Solution'.[12]

In 1986, coming back to the subject forty years after his first youthful assessment, Mandel tried to meet this test – in his book on the Second World War. Even here the first signs are not propitious. Only three pages are devoted by him to the Holocaust, and the context plainly renders it a subordinate issue. For his discussion of it occurs in a country-by-country survey of *ideology* within the major arenas of the war. The fate of European Jewry figures only as part of this survey. The discussion nevertheless marks a definite development of Mandel's viewpoint as compared with his essay of 1946. No longer is it only 'material interests', capitalist economy and crisis, that are at work. His explanation of the Holocaust now combines a particular form of ideology on the one hand, with features of capitalist modernity on the other. The ideology is racism. This, Mandel argues, is 'congenitally linked to institutionalized colonialism and imperialism', owing to the need with these political and economic formations to dehumanize whole groups of people in order to rationalize and justify oppressing them in extreme ways. It is then a short step from there, from dehumanizing them, to denying such groups the right to life itself. When racist ideology combines with the global irrationality of capitalism and its '"perfect" local rationality' – what Mandel calls also 'the deadly partial rationality of the modern industrial system' – that step, according to him, 'is frequently taken'.

12. Ibid., pp. 12, 17. And cf. Ernest Mandel, 'Der Mensch ist das Höchste Wesen für den Menschen', in F. J. Raddatz, ed., *Warum Ich Marxist Bin*, Frankfurt 1980: 'The great intellectual attraction of Marxism lies in its (up till now unique) ability to achieve a rational, all-inclusive and coherent integration of all social sciences'; 'It is . . . in the final analysis the science of mankind *tout court*'. Quoted from a typescript translation in the author's possession, made by Jurrian Bendien.

Further, a number of additional factors, political and psychological, are brought in by Mandel to account for the particular result that was the Nazi genocide. Amongst these factors are: a desperado elite holding political power; the *va banque* aggression unleashed by it in conjunction with sectors of big business; a policy of state terrorism with 'an implacable logic of its own'; the passive complicity of thousands of people, civil servants and other executive agents; and 'a fetid substratum of unconscious guilt and shame'.[13] I shall come back to the significance of these other factors. But clearly there has been an inner differentiation and some filling out of Mandel's thinking on this question, as one would expect from a writer of now greater maturity. I find, all the same, that the key problems are unresolved.

First, Mandel offers precious little sense, and certainly no attempt at an elaboration, of the singularity or specificity of the Shoah. On the contrary, the overwhelming weight of his emphasis is, once again, on contextualizing it – on its comparability with other historical phenomena. We are referred by him to 'the mass enslavement and killing of Blacks via the slave trade' and to the extermination of Indians by the *conquistadors*; to the fact that gypsies and 'sections of the Slav people' also figured on the list of the Nazis' victims, as did tens of thousands of ethnic Germans murdered in the T4 (so-called 'euthanasia') programme; to the Japanese atrocities in 'Unit 731' in Manchuria, 'only one rung below Auschwitz'; to the bombing of Hiroshima and Nagasaki, reflecting a contempt for human beings 'not far removed from extreme racism'; and to the fact that anti-semitism and other Nazi attitudes were and are widespread beyond Germany.

True, Mandel also writes this: 'the Holocaust – the delib-

13. See Ernest Mandel, *The Meaning of the Second World War*, London 1986, pp. 90–92. Reference to Mandel's views in the paragraphs following is to these pages until otherwise indicated.

erate and systematic killing of six million men, women and children simply because of their ethnic origin – stands as a unique crime in mankind's sad criminal history'. But that is all he writes. And it is not now clear in what the Holocaust *is* unique, if it is.

I do not want to be misunderstood. I am not suggesting that the Jewish tragedy is not at all, not in any way, comparable to other great horrors and crimes. Of course it is. But these are the respective weights Mandel gives to the two sides of the question: several paragraphs on the comparability of the tragedy; a single, unexplicated sentence on its specificity or uniqueness. This is a much debated and difficult question within a now very extensive literature (though, like many of the other difficult questions there, it is not one much reflected on by Marxists). The historian Yehuda Bauer has proposed in connection with it the metaphor of a huge volcano rising out of a dark, forbidding landscape: the volcano is part of the landscape; but it also stands out against it.[14] Mandel says much about the landscape ('mankind's sad criminal history') and about the Holocaust's being part of this. He says nearly nothing about the Holocaust standing out. Or he says only *that* it stands out, but not how.

Second, Mandel is extremely confident of the power of social and political explanation here. Referring to 'those who have treated Hitler's fanatic anti-semitism leading to the Holocaust as beyond rational explanation', he writes that 'such drastic historical exceptionalism' cannot be sustained – then going on to proffer the explanation I have summarized. Now, again, in order to avoid being misunderstood, let me say that I do not support any radical incomprehensibility thesis. The attempt to destroy the Jews was an event in history, and its preconditions, causes, processes, can and must be investigated with a view to trying to understand

14. *The Holocaust in Historical Perspective*, pp. 37–8.

them. In this matter more perhaps than any other we need to understand as much as we can, so as to be able to resist as well as we can all further projects of mass murder and appalling cruelty. However, the sort of opinion I have quoted from Isaac Deutscher (and which is shared by many others) expresses the sense, even if sometimes exaggerated, that there is a residue within this historical experience beyond the regular forms of social, political or ideological explanation: a residue which is called by Deutscher baffling, and 'degeneration of the human character', and called by other people other things. Mandel seems to give it no legitimate place. This will become clearer in light of my last critical point.

Which is that, third, for all the greater complexity of his analysis at this later date, the Holocaust is still presented by him as being an effect of *capitalism*; as the product of its global irrationality, its partial (functional) rationality, and the racist ideology generated by its imperialist forms. But this explanation does not suffice to its object, no more than do explanations of the catastrophe as a product of modernity. Faced with either one or the other we may legitimately ask why, in view of the generality of the social condition invoked as primary to the event, *this* has happened so far only once. (The question should not be taken to imply that the structures of capitalism or of modernity do not have any important part in an overall explanation.) In truth, Mandel is obliged for greater completeness to bring in as factors of his own explanation less class-specific and capitalism-specific causes, both motivational and political: such as the servile complicity and lack of critical judgement of tens of thousands of people; unconscious guilt and shame; extreme policy choices with a dynamic of their own; and indeed dehumanization itself, now become a central category and for its part a rather widespread and familiar human disposition. But none of this is recognized by Mandel as having broadened the scope of the analysis to encompass more general, less historically specific themes – perhaps even to the point where a residue of sheer, ungrounded excess may remain.

This failure to recognize the now broader nature of his analysis is highlighted by one startling and cavalier judgement which he allows himself. Having got to the end of his multi-factor exposition of what led to the Jewish catastrophe – not only extreme racism and the irrationality of capitalism, coupled with its functional, industrial rationality, but also widespread complicity, a desperado political elite, its *va banque* policy of aggression, a state terrorism with its own logic, and then an unconscious layer of guilt and shame as well – Mandel comments:

> The Holocaust only comes at the end of this long causal chain. But it can and must be explained through it. Indeed, *those who understood the chain were able to foresee it.* (Emphasis added.)

The reference here is to Trotsky's prediction from which we began, and to me this is a *reductio ad absurdum* of the totalizing ambition of Mandel's approach: attempting to 'recover' the heterogeneity in the explanation by treating everything in it as part of one unified chain, and then imagining that Trotsky's 1938 prediction might really have been based on being able to foresee all the individual links in it *and* their connection. I cannot take the suggestion seriously. Especially not, remembering the context of general unpreparedness and incredulity vis-à-vis the Jewish calamity as it first loomed and then became a reality. Trotsky would have needed to be superhuman to have had this much understanding in advance. I think we have to look, rather, towards a looser kind of foresight on his part, although coming together this, needless to say, with his Marxist knowledge of the grave dangers of capitalist crisis and of the typical conflicts it throws up and the ugly new forms it can breed.

Intimations of what I am getting at in speaking of this looser kind of foresight are to be found in observations Ernest Mandel himself made about Trotsky, both earlier and later. Earlier, in his study of him already referred to, Mandel writes that Trotsky understood 'the fact that irrational ideas, moods and yearnings of great force had survived from pre-capitalist times in large parts of bourgeois society'; and that though racism is a typical ideology of the colonial-imperialist epoch it is combined with 'remnants of pre-bourgeois ideology'.[15] Later, in *Trotsky As Alternative* (first published in German in 1992), he repeats this latter point. And he says also that Trotsky saw fascist ideology and rule as involving, at one and the same time, a 'relapse into pre-capitalist reaction and obscurantism' and a late, catching-up form of modernization.[16]

Many of you will be familiar with the better known passages on which Mandel here draws; passages, in particular, from the article of 1933, 'What is National Socialism?'. In this, Trotsky characterizes Nazi ideology as a reaction against the rationalism and materialism of the last two centuries, and as integrating a pogromist anti-semitism into the defence of capitalism against the threat represented by the working class. He goes on to talk of 'the depths of society' having been opened up; of 'inexhaustible reserves ... of darkness, ignorance, and savagery'. And he says that what should have been eliminated as excrement from the national organism with 'the normal development' of society 'has now come gushing out from the throat; capitalist society is puking up the undigested barbarism. Such is the physiology of National Socialism'.[17] It is a repugnant image but in its own way also a

15. *Trotsky: A Study* . . . , pp. 89–90.
16. Ernest Mandel, *Trotsky As Alternative*, London 1995, p. 108.
17. *The Struggle Against Fascism in Germany*, pp. 403–5.

prophetic one. Undigested barbarism. Its final consequences of a darkness inexhaustible indeed. Trotsky would later, in a manifesto of the Fourth International on the war, describe fascism 'as a chemically pure distillation of the culture of imperialism', with anti-semitism a stable element within the racial themes of Nazi propaganda and belief.[18]

Now, in an illuminating analysis of the development of Trotsky's thinking on the Jewish question, Enzo Traverso has presented us with an evolution broadly as follows: from anti-semitism being seen by him initially as a feudal survival in the process of dying out, to a later appreciation of its significance as a symptom of capitalist crisis and modernist barbarism. Anti-semitism within Nazi ideology, Traverso proposes likewise, was at first viewed by Trotsky as part of an obscurantist reaction to modernity, then later understood as an authentic expression of contemporary capitalism and imperialism.[19] While there is a clear textual basis for this interpretation,[20] nevertheless I think, myself, that in his emphasis on the change in Trotsky's thinking Traverso bypasses the importance of the *combination* (of new and old ideological forms) that some of Mandel's quoted formulas bring out. The continuity – and so susceptibility to such combination – between pre-modern and modern forms may be highlighted in two ways.

Consider, first, the category of dehumanization, become pivotal to Mandel's account. Undoubtedly a development occurs between older forms of Christian anti-semitism and the Nazi, racial, variant of it. However, whether the Jews are seen as refusing the truth they themselves had anticipated, as God-killers and in some sort a demonic influence, or are

---

18. *On the Jewish Question*, pp. 30–31 – and cf. p. 20.
19. Enzo Traverso, 'Trotsky et la question juive', *Quatrième Internationale* 36 (1990), pp. 76–8; and his *Les Marxistes et la question juive*, Montreuil 1990, pp. 155–6, 219–22.
20. See the references given in footnote 18 above.

seen rather as beings of a biologically inferior type, they are placed at the margins of, or actually excluded from, the sphere of the fully human and from the reciprocal moral consideration associated with it. Nazi popular attitudes were certainly hybrid here, drawing on long-standing Christian prejudices and linking these with a pseudo-scientific racial theory. More generally, it is hard to believe that just *any* people could have been as murderously dealt with over a whole continent, or as readily abandoned to its torment, rather than this particular people, hated and vilified there for going-on two millennia. The psychological distancing effected by fixing others as in one way or another menacingly alien is at any rate an age-old symbolic mechanism. It has a transhistorical dimension.

Similarly, the content of the category of barbarism as used by Mandel and other Marxists (whether wittingly or not) is of a highly generic kind, and is, I would suggest, essentially anthropological. The category is used to refer loosely to such phenomena as obsessive, unreasoning hatreds, extreme or endemic violence, the enjoyment of cruelty, indifference to great suffering and so forth. None of this is specific to capitalism.

The centrality of such categories to Mandel's understanding of the Holocaust indicates why it is not genuinely containable by an explanation in terms of the socio-economic and ideological forms of capitalism. I shall come to an elaboration of this point by way of examining his last and most developed attempt to grapple with the issue. I mean the article of 1990, 'Prémisses matérielles, sociales et idéologiques du génocide nazi'. (In discussing it I shall make supplementary reference also to an appendix Mandel wrote for the German edition of his book on the Second World War, published just one year later than this article. What is relevant in the appendix for the most part reproduces the theses of the article. So far as it differs from it in one interesting respect, I shall speak of the difference later, in concluding.) The central strands and weaknesses of Mandel's approach in this article remain basically unchanged. But it represents, all the same, a further development of his thinking, because the residual factors in the explanation have been reinforced. I shall take these two sets of features of the article in turn.

We still find here just a couple of brief phrases on the singularity of the Holocaust. Mandel writes of it as 'a unique event in history up to now', and as involving 'the worst crimes in history'. His reasons for the judgement remain to be clearly spelled out.[21] The 'contextualizing' material, on the other hand, is rather fuller. We are reminded with a multiplicity of references – to slavery in the ancient world, the persecution of witches, the fate of the American Indians, black slavery; and to the murder of gypsies, Poles and Russians during the Second World War – that, whether as victims *tout court* or as victims of the Nazis, the Jews belong to a very much larger company.[22] Who amongst serious people is in need of this reminder?

Then, too, Mandel continues to reject as (without qualification) 'obscurantist' the view that the Holocaust is incomprehensible. I return shortly to a claim he makes in that connection.[23] And the key to his own explanation remains what it was before. The Holocaust is to be understood as 'the most extreme expression to this point of the destructive tendencies present in bourgeois society'.[24] It is the product of a biological racism itself arising from socio-economic practices that require the systematic dehumanization of

21. Ernest Mandel, 'Prémisses matérielles, sociales et idéologiques du génocide nazi', in Y. Thanassekos and H. Wismann, eds., *Révision de l'histoire*, Paris 1990 (pp. 169–74), sections 1 and 11. All references to this text will be given so, by section number.
22. Ibid., sections 2, 3.
23. Ibid., section 11.
24. Ibid., section 10.

other peoples; linked, this, to that 'typical combination of partial perfect rationality and global irrationality ... characteristic of bourgeois society'; in conditions, generally, of the crisis of imperialism; and conditions, specifically, of a profound social and political crisis in the given (that is, German) national arena.[25]

That all this is to the point is one thing. That it fully captures its intended object is another. It does not. We begin to see why by looking at what Mandel throws in here, sometimes just by the way, as additional factors: factors of a psychological, ethical and experiential nature.

Thus, first, in connection with dehumanizing racist ideologies that rationalize the mistreatment of other human beings, he speaks of a need, consequent upon such mistreatment, for '"neutralizing" bad conscience and the feeling of individual guilt' – but without any further enlargement.[26] Second, in connection with the Nazi policy of extermination having 'begun with the Jews', Mandel gives as a partial cause of this 'the lunatic belief of Hitler and some of his lieutenants in an "international Jewish conspiracy"'.[27] Third, there is a passing reference to the First World War as an event without which Nazism as a mass phenomenon would have been unthinkable. In the aforementioned appendix to the German edition of his book on the Second World War, Mandel deals with the same point at greater length and says that 'the chauvinist enthusiasm [of 1914] ... the acceptance of senseless mass killings and boundless destruction constitute the great break in contemporary history. This was the

25. See in turn, ibid., sections 1, 6, 5, and 8; and also, on the rationality/ irrationality combination, Mandel's appendix ('Zum Historikerstreit') to his *Der Zweite Weltkrieg*, Frankfurt 1991, at pp. 224–5.
26. 'Prémisses', section 1. And cf. 'Zum Historikerstreit', p. 220: 'An investigation of this sort ... should by no means rule out consideration of ideological, and mass-psychological as well as individual-psychological, factors in the chain of causation'.
27. 'Prémisses', section 3.

first decisive step towards barbarism ...'[28] Is there not an important insight here? The suggestion may be speculative, but could not this trauma of mass death, this prolonged, unprecedentedly large and useless slaughter, with its scarring effects on the consciousness of a generation, have had some part in preparing the 'moral' ground for the genocide to follow?

However that may be, Mandel addresses himself also, fourth, and perhaps most crucially in this context, to reasons for the Jewish tragedy 'of an ethical order': to do with the complicity and obedience – and whether on account of routine, self-interested calculation or cowardice – of millions of Europeans, ordinary people accepting the authority of the State rather than 'the fundamental rules of ethics'. He concludes in this regard, 'In the face of massive injustice, individual and above all collective resistance and revolt are not only a right but a duty ... That is the principal lesson of the Holocaust.'[29]

In touching on such matters Ernest Mandel connects to a wider historiographical, socio-psychological and other litera-ture on the Holocaust, adding to it, to be sure, what Marxism is best-placed to add. He connects there also to another layer of human understandings *as well as* difficulties of understand-ing. It is doubtful these can be easily recuperated within a crisis-of-capitalism type of explanation as it is Mandel's constant tendency to try to recuperate everything.

For think of it now: bad conscience and guilt. Think, even in terms of quite ordinary experience, of some of the behaviours this can produce. Think of *lunatic* beliefs and what they can produce. Think of mass death and those who take part in the experience of it, and of those who have to cope emotionally with its enduring effects. Think of moral

28. Ibid., section 5; and 'Zum Historikerstreit', pp. 229–30.
29. 'Prémisses', section 7; and cf. 'Zum Historikerstreit', p. 232.

cowardice or merely moral 'slippage', of failure to act against
known wrongs and of the many different ways there are of
living comfortably with that. We begin to reach into the sub-
soil, so to say, of the human psyche. And we are not so far,
surely, from Deutscher's 'degeneration of the human character'. But for Deutscher something here was still baffling
where for Mandel, seemingly, everything is clear. The former
view for many people has appeared to be more persuasive:
that, in the excess, the passage to the limit of what the 'Final
Solution of the Jewish Question' envisaged, indeed the
passage in the execution of it beyond every familiar limit,
there was something which eludes historical understanding
and social scientific explanation. You can spell out all the
conditions, factors, contributory causes; still, these were not
bound to produce exactly *that*. By themselves, therefore, they
do not altogether explain it.

One especially influential voice has argued to this effect. I
refer to Primo Levi. Levi wrote that the commonly accepted
explanations did not satisfy him. 'They are reductive; not
commensurate with, nor proportionate to, the facts that
need explaining ... I cannot avoid the impression of a
general atmosphere of uncontrolled madness that seems to
me to be unique in history.' For Levi, multi-factor explanations were necessary but they also fell short. He preferred,
he said, the humility of those historians who 'confess to *not
understanding*', to not understanding *such* a furious hatred. It
was, Levi wrote, 'a poison fruit sprung from the deadly trunk
of Fascism, but outside of and beyond Fascism itself'.[30]

In his 'Premisses' essay, Mandel seeks to fend off views of
this kind with the argument that they generalize responsibility for evil to humanity at large, in effect accusing everybody and consequently nobody in particular, not Hitler, nor

30. Primo Levi, Afterword to *If This is a Man and The Truce*, London 1987,
pp. 394–6.

the Nazis, nor their supporters.[31] But to me this is an obvious *non sequitur*, not worth lingering over. That we may not be able to comprehend everything about the calamity visited on the Jews in no way entails that we are then unable to see any difference between the innocent and the guilty.

I come back now to Trotsky's remarkable prediction of 1938 and I ask again: what was its basis? Doubtless his Marxist understanding of the dangers of fascism in general and of German National Socialism in particular had something to do with it. But this on its own could not have sufficed to yield the extremity within the prediction he made. I want to suggest that there was an element of plain intuition here, spun from Trotsky's broader human sensibility in which something was already known about 'uncontrolled madness', deadly hatred and the passing of all limits. Of this broader sensibility one could cite much evidence. It is what made Trotsky the powerful and creative Marxist intellect he was, his many calumniators notwithstanding. But I shall cite only a single relevant piece which I have had occasion to draw attention to once before.[32]

It is an account of a pogrom from his book *1905*, an episode narrated there of the failed Russian revolution of that year. Describing the build-up to the pogrom, Trotsky – Marxist – sketches both its political background and something of the social composition of the mob. Then he writes this: 'the gang rushes through the town, drunk on vodka and the smell of blood.' Drunk *on the smell of blood*. What specifically Marxist category is there for that? Trotsky relates:

Everything is allowed to him [the member of the gang], he is capable of anything, he is the master of property and honour, of life

31. 'Prémisses', section 11.
32. See Norman Geras, 'Literature of Revolution', *New Left Review* 113–114 (January/April 1979), pp. 25–29; reprinted in my collection, *Literature of Revolution*, London 1986, at pp. 247–50.

and death ... If he wants to, he can throw an old woman out of a third-floor window together with a grand piano, he can smash a chair against a baby's head, rape a little girl while the entire crowd looks on, hammer a nail into a living human body ... He exterminates whole families, he pours petrol over a house, transforms it into a mass of flames, and if anyone attempts to escape, he finishes him off with a cudgel ... There exist no tortures, figments of a feverish brain maddened by alcohol and fury, at which he need ever stop. He is capable of anything, he dares everything ...

And Trotsky goes on:

> The victims, bloodstained, charred, driven frantic, still search for salvation within the nightmare. Some put on the bloodstained clothes of people already dead, lie down in a pile of corpses ... Others fall on their knees before the officers, the policemen, the raider, they stretch out their arms, crawl in the dust, kiss the soldiers' boots, beg for mercy. In reply they hear only drunken laughter. 'You wanted freedom? Here, look, this is it.'

In these last mocking words, Trotsky says, 'is contained the whole infernal morality of the pogrom policy'; and he repeats once again, 'capable of everything'.[33]

Already long before 1938 Trotsky had seen into the depths. He had seen the spirit of limitless excess, the exaltation people can feel in exercising a merciless power over others and the 'total-ness' there can be in a humiliation – both the horror and the joy that is taken in inflicting it, lethal couple in what is already an annihilation. He had seen also one of the more terrifying faces of human freedom, self-consciously turned against its other, better faces. In all of this he had seen part of what there would subsequently be in the Shoah, including the element of an irreducible choice. The preconditions and the surrounding context of this kind of

33. Leon Trotsky, *1905*, London 1972, pp. 131–5.

choice can and always must be explored and described. But it remains in the end what it is: underdetermined, a choice.

Whether or not there was in Trotsky's mental processes any direct route running from the memory of his earlier description of a pogrom to predicting in 1938 the physical extermination of the Jews cannot, of course, be known. I simply offer as a hypothesis that it was out of the kind of understanding which that narrative of his betokens, as much as it was out of his Marxist theorizing about capitalism or fascism, that his anticipation of Nazism's ultimate barbarity may have come. What he wrote there in any case foreshadows themes that were to be proposed later by others in thinking about the Shoah itself. I want to mention two of these others.

Saul Friedlander has written of a feeling evident alike within the Nazi leadership and amongst some of its followers, 'of accomplishing something truly, historically, meta-historically, exceptional'; a feeling manifested, for example, in 'the insistence of some of the commanders of the *Einsatzgruppen* [engaged in the mass murder of Jews by shooting] to stay on duty'.[34] Developing the point he has argued that, beyond the undeniable explanatory importance of anti-semitic ideology and the dynamics of bureaucracy, there is also 'an independent psychological residue [that] seems to defy the historian'. It concerns, Friedlander says, 'a compelling lust for killing on an immense scale, driven by some kind of extraordinary elation ...' And it is just here, with this elation, that 'our understanding remains blocked on the level of self-awareness':

> The historian can analyse the phenomenon from the 'outside', but ... his unease stems from the noncongruence between intellectual probing and the blocking of intuitive comprehension ...[35]

34. See Martin Broszat/Saul Friedlander, 'A Controversy about the Historiciza-tion of National Socialism', *Yad Vashem Studies* 19 (1988), pp. 28–9.
35. Saul Friedlander, 'The "Final Solution": On the Unease in Historical

Friedlander reads such a feeling of elation in a notorious speech of Himmler's before a gathering of SS officers, at which the Nazi leader praised the magnitude of their accomplishment in the destruction of the Jews. The same thing can be read, repeatedly, in testimonies from those present at the sites of mass murder.

The elation and the lust for killing. A battalion of German reserve policemen on duty in Poland and drafted into rounding up and shooting Jews is enjoying a visit from an entertainment unit from Berlin. 'The members of this unit had ... heard of the pending shooting of the Jews. They asked, indeed even emphatically begged, to be allowed to participate in the execution of the Jews.'[36] Again: 'Members of the Grenzpolizeikommissariat were, with a few exceptions, quite happy to take part in shootings of Jews. They had a ball! ... Nobody failed to turn up.' 'As usual a few of the new officers became megalomaniacs, they really enter into the role wholeheartedly.' '... after a while we saw numerous soldiers and civilians pouring on to an embankment in front of us, behind which ... executions were being carried out at regular intervals.' '... some marines from the naval unit came past ... they had heard that Jews were always being shot in the town and ... they wanted to see this for themselves ... The execution area was visited by scores of German spectators from the Navy and the Reichsbahn (railway).' 'I saw SD personnel weeping because they could not cope mentally with what was going on. Then again I encountered others who kept a score-sheet of how many

Interpretation', in Peter Hayes, ed., *Lessons and Legacies: The Meaning of the Holocaust in a Changing World*, Evanston 1991, pp. 23–35, at pp. 25, 30–31. The essay is reprinted, slightly modified, in Friedlander's *Memory, History, and the Extermination of the Jews of Europe*, Bloomington 1993, pp. 102–16.
36. Christopher R. Browning, *Ordinary Men: Reserve Police Battalion 101 and the Final Solution in Poland*, New York 1993, p. 112.

people they had sent to their death.'[37] Or here, a Norwegian imprisoned at Sachsenhausen describes a group of young Germans let loose with truncheons on hundreds of starving Jews: '[T]he act of striking intoxicated them and drove them wild ... they were living devils, possessed, transported with ecstasy ... they went on striking at them as they lay, trod upon them, kicked them, while the blood was streaming from mouths, ears, and wounds. Every time they needed a rest, they turned exultantly to their laughing and smiling comrades, laughed back, and gave the truncheon a limber, playful swing round their heads. Then they flew at it again.'[38]

The critic George Steiner, like Friedlander acknowledging the importance of what has been explained of this historical experience by the various disciplines of empirical enquiry, suggests that these have been unable nonetheless to fathom the intensity of the hatreds that were unleashed, or to account for the extreme lengths to which the Nazis were willing to go in pursuit of their murderous objective. In a thesis he concedes to be unprovable, Steiner argues that it might have been as the inventors of monotheism, of 'an infinite ... ethically imperative God', that the Jews drew upon themselves all the furies released in the course of the Nazi-led assault against them. Representing what he calls the 'blackmail of perfection', they perhaps incurred a hatred the more intense because of a recognition at some level by their tormentors of the desirability of the ethical demands embodied in the Jewish tradition.[39] The thesis is of a guilt turned outwards, of resentment focused on a people which had

37. Ernst Klee, Willi Dressen and Volker Riess, eds., 'Those were the Days': The Holocaust through the Eyes of the Perpetrators and Bystanders, London 1991, pp. 76, 89, 118, 127, 129.
38. Odd Nansen, From Day to Day, New York 1949, p. 438.
39. George Steiner, 'The Long Life of Metaphor: An Approach to the "Shoah"', in Berel Lang, ed., Writing and the Holocaust, New York 1988, pp. 154–71, at pp. 161–6. The article is reprinted from Encounter 68 (February 1987), pp. 55–61.

thought to make itself the bearer of hope for a better world. It recalls hints we have encountered in Mandel and Trotsky: the former's allusion to bad conscience; the scene narrated by the latter of a freedom not liberating, but cruelly, wilfully, destructive. Unprovable as Steiner's thesis may be and in manifest tension even with other more familiar, dehumanizing and demonizing tropes, it is hard, I believe, to refuse it any weight once one has absorbed from the vast chronicle of this catastrophe the sense that is so pervasively present in it of a determination by the perpetrators, a glee almost, in taking advantage of the innocence, vulnerability, persistent hope and propensity to think in terms of what was reasonable, of their targeted victims.

Whatever the sources of the anti-Jewish fury, and they are probably multiple, no one reading at all widely in the testimony and historiography of the Holocaust could fail to notice what both Friedlander and Steiner speak of in their different ways, neither the cruel desires and sense of an unusual elation, nor the emotional charge produced – and maybe required – by the assault upon the innocent. Such features are obscured, however, in a certain body of the theoretical literature by alternative discourses there. One of these is the 'banality of evil' argument, due originally to Hannah Arendt but disseminated very widely since. The other, frequently related to it, is a broader argument about modernity to be found in the work of many different writers.

Both of these arguments register things that are important to understanding the Nazi genocide. In a nutshell, the first draws attention to the general normality of the perpetrators from a psychological point of view: to their kinship with the rest of humankind as, mostly, ordinary people, not monsters and, especially, not animals. The second argument draws attention to the characteristically modern structures and resources, social, organizational and technical, without which an enterprise of this type and scale – gathering and transporting six million people from across the countries of Europe in order to kill them all, and this within a period of less than four years and under a blanket of attempted secrecy – would have been much more difficult, if not actually impossible. But despite the pertinence of these arguments, they can come, when given a too unilateral emphasis, to present a picture of rule-governed, bureaucratic murder in which some of the other aspects we have been concerned with, symbolic, emotional and to do with the unfettered 'play' of destructive human capacity and imagination, are all but marginalized. There is something here that is not about modernity; something that is not about capitalism either. It is about humanity.

It is something that Marxists have often been reluctant to face up to but with which – returning now to him – Ernest Mandel ought to have had no trouble. In an essay of 1980 entitled 'Man is the supreme being for man', he wrote of there being anthropological constants. One such constant was expressed in a yearning for freedom and in 'the inextinguishable spark of revolt' against injustice and oppression. But there were also, Mandel recognized, 'deeply embedded in human beings', impulses towards tribalism and destructiveness.[40]

Confronted with the enormities produced by these latter kind of impulses, the better side of human nature that is represented by impulses of the former kind can find itself, it seems, at a loss – as to how to understand. This is what Deutscher and Levi and Friedlander all tell us, each in his own particular accents. It is good that human beings experience the difficulty as widely as they do. Should we ever entirely cease to, we would be entirely lost. This, for its part, is the meaning – an ethical rather than psychological meaning – of the discourse of the *monstrosity* of radical evil.

* * *

40. See the reference given in footnote 12 above.

I want, finally, to note a respect in which, in the pages he appended to the German edition of his book on the Second World War, Mandel found it necessary to express himself more fully than he had ever done before. It was on the issue of the uniqueness of the Jewish calamity. I conclude with some observations arising from a certain change of emphasis about this.

Hitherto, at least after the initial article of 1946, although Mandel characterizes the Holocaust as unique (and not in any trivially individuating sense but in the sense, as we have seen, of uniquely criminal, worst), he does so without spelling out the reasons for his view. The texts we have so far considered oblige us to rely on the briefest of indications to gather what those reasons might be. Thus, in both *The Meaning of the Second World War* and in his 'Premisses' essay, he refers to the systematic nature of the killing. Other comments made by him suggest that 'systematic' might unpack into two features commonly cited in debates on this question, features which we may label, for short, *modernity* and *comprehensiveness of intent.* Mandel writes that the perpetrators of earlier massacres were not more humane than the perpetrators of this one; it is just that 'their means and plans ... were more limited'. And he writes of the Jews being killed 'simply' on account of their ethnic origin.[41] Is it, then, because of the modern methods applied to their murder and because the intention of the Nazis was a total one, to kill them all, that the crime against the European Jews is to be seen as a *novum* morally speaking?

It turns out to be so. Such is what Mandel now puts forward in a more explicit and elaborated way in this German appendix. He begins with a description of the crime as the 'systematic, carefully planned and rapidly industrial-

41. *The Meaning of the Second World War*, p. 92; 'Prémisses', section 2. And see also, with respect to comprehensiveness of intent, *Trotsky As Alternative*, p. 155, note 25.

ized' murder of six million people for the 'single reason [of] their supposed descent', and he goes on to present a version of the modernity thesis, a version of it of strong Marxist coloration. This emphasizes, on the one hand, the technical, administrative and division of labour aspects of the genocide, and its dependence on the railways and the chemical and building industries. And it insists on the part played, on the other hand, by 'the "basic moral values" of the ruling class': a pervasive mentality of obedience to the state, patriotism, nationalism and conformity. It was such organizational structures and such attitudes making for passive complicity that were, according to Mandel, decisive; as much as it was fanatical anti-semitism and much more than it was any 'moral nihilism'.[42]

Now, there are some difficult and unpleasant questions here about why these features, whether separately or jointly, should distinguish the Holocaust as uniquely bad – questions about the normative comparison of evils that I will have to leave to one side. I intend to address them on another occasion.[43] It is interesting, however, to consider why it should have been just at this juncture, in this particular text, that Mandel endeavoured at last to lay out more fully the view that the Holocaust was unique, where before the weight of his emphasis had been much more upon its comparability with other historical experiences. Naturally, it is hard to be

42. 'Zum Historikerstreit', pp. 209, 222–3.
43. There is also the explanatory question already once mooted. Mandel is unable to account even for the unique features of the event as he identifies these, since neither the structures nor the mentalities he focuses on seem to suffice, given their pervasiveness in the modern world, to the extremity of what occurred. He is aware of the problem, for he sets himself to trying to respond to it: to explaining what it was that produced the specific outcome from these more general tendencies. (See ibid., pp. 240–43.) But his response – in terms of the failure of the German bourgeois revolution, the rapid growth of German industry and the ambitions of German imperialism for a redivision of existing spheres of influence – seems to me to fall far short of the thing it purports to address. None of these causes speaks directly to the aim of *wiping out a people*.

sure about the answer, but I would venture that the literary context is significant: an afterword for a German audience, in the wake of the recent 'Historikerstreit' (the historian's controversy), and dealing with the views of Ernst Nolte and their manifest tendency to apologia.

What follows should only be said bluntly. Within this apologia there is a standpoint bearing a formal resemblance to something I have criticized in Mandel. I mean the energetic contextualization of Nazi crimes by Nolte, even while briefly conceding their singular and unprecedented character: his insistence that they belong to the same history of modern times as the American war in Vietnam, the Vietnamese invasion of Cambodia, the exodus from Vietnam of the boat people – a 'holocaust on the water' – the Cambodian genocide, the repression following on the Iranian revolution, the Soviet invasion of Afghanistan and, above all, the liquidation of the kulaks, and the Gulag. Against that backdrop, Nolte urged that the Third Reich 'should be removed from the isolation in which it still finds itself.'[44] This is what came, in the debate in question, to be called 'relativization' of the Holocaust; and it is what Mandel himself calls it in taking issue with Nolte's views.[45] He (Mandel) continues even now to assert that the Holocaust was an extreme product of tendencies which are historically more general.[46] But he perceives a need, evidently, to balance the assertion with a greater emphasis on the singularity of the fate of the Jews.

On this matter especially, let there be no misunderstanding. I speak of a formal resemblance. But the same moral

44. Ernst Nolte, 'Between Historical Myth and Revisionism?' and 'A Past That Will Not Pass Away', *Yad Vashem Studies* 19 (1988), pp. 49–63 and 65–73. Also in J. Knowlton and T. Cates (translators), *Forever in the Shadow of Hitler?*, Atlantic Highlands 1993, pp. 1–15 and 18–23.
45. 'Zum Historikerstreit', p. 209.
46. Ibid., pp. 239, 242, 245.

significance is not to be attached to the two standpoints formally alike: that of a German conservative historian and that of a Jewish Marxist revolutionary. For what motivated their respective emphases was not the same. A national particularism concerned with 'normalizing' Germany's modern historical identity was plainly at work in the first case. And the very opposite was probably at the root of the second, a socialist and in its way Jewish universalism that would not risk belittling the sufferings of others by dwelling too emphatically on the tragedy of the Jews.

It is an old story of socialism, going a long way back. It was represented by a figure of great importance for Mandel, of great importance for him in many respects, but one of these in having voiced the clearest of warnings about capitalist barbarism. From prison during the First World War, Rosa Luxemburg wrote to her friend Mathilde Wurm:

> What do you want with this particular suffering of the Jews? The poor victims on the rubber plantations in Putumayo, the Negroes in Africa with whose bodies the Europeans play a game of catch, are just as near to me. Do you remember the words written on the work of the Great General Staff about Trotha's campaign in the Kalahari desert? 'And the death-rattles, the mad cries of those dying of thirst, faded away into the sublime silence of eternity.' Oh, this 'sublime silence of eternity' in which so many screams have faded away unheard. It rings within me so strongly that I have no special corner of my heart reserved for the ghetto: I am at home wherever in the world there are clouds, birds and human tears.[47]

An old story of socialism and an old story of Jews on the left, and these words of Rosa Luxemburg are excellent ones, not to be forgotten or renounced, especially not today. Still, in the second half of the twentieth century, they are also less than adequate. A Jewish socialist ought to be able to find

47. Stephen Eric Bronner, ed., *The Letters of Rosa Luxemburg*, Boulder 1978, pp. 179–80.

some special corner of his or her heart for the tragedy of the Jewish people. A universalist ethic shorn of any special concern for the sufferings of one's own would be the less persuasive for such carelessness. Whatever one may think about that, a balance is at any rate called for in estimating the place – comparable *and* unique – of the Shoah.

I take one last precaution to avoid the risk of an imbalance here myself. Writing about the Jewish question, both Mandel and Trotsky argued that there could be no satisfactory resolution of it except through the achievement of social-ism.[48] All of the foregoing indicates, I hope, the shortcomings I see in that formula. Nevertheless, it secretes a certain truth as well. If we generalize from the so-called Jewish question to other cases of extreme persecution and oppression, the link which has so often been made by the political tradition of Mandel, Trotsky and Luxemburg, the link between capital-ism and barbarism, is not to be lightly shrugged aside. Capitalism is a social and economic order systematically producing for millions of people – and all confident contem-porary liberalisms notwithstanding – conditions of extreme want and oppression, in which hatreds are the more likely to accumulate, fester, erupt. It encourages moral attitudes, moreover, that may be described as underwriting a 'contract of mutual indifference': under which people in acute danger or trouble may be simply left there, so far as their situation is considered to be the business of anyone else. Not responsible for all evil, capitalist social relations and values contribute their massive share to it. Socialism represents the hope of another moral universe, one in which, to advert again to Mandel's 'principal lesson of the Holocaust', there might

48. See Trotsky, *On the Jewish Question*, pp. 18–22, 28–9; Germain [Mandel], 'La question juive au lendemain de la deuxième guerre mondiale', p. XII; and Ernest Germain, 'A Biographical Sketch of Abram Leon', in Abram Leon, *The Jewish Question: A Marxist Interpretation*, New York 1970, p. 17.

come to be enough people no longer willing to tolerate the morally intolerable that the instances of this could be at last radically reduced. It is to that vision that, balanced or not on any particular question, Mandel devoted his life.

Bibliography

Theodor Adorno, *Negative Dialectics*, Routledge, London 1973.

Jean Améry, *At the Mind's Limits: Contemplations by a Survivor on Auschwitz and its Realities*, Schocken, New York 1990.

Hannah Arendt, *Eichmann in Jerusalem*, Penguin, London 1977.

W. H. Auden, *Collected Shorter Poems 1927–1957*, Faber, London 1969.

David Bankier, 'The Germans and the Holocaust: What Did They Know?', *Yad Vashem Studies* 20 (1990).

Yehuda Bauer, *The Holocaust in Historical Perspective*, University of Washington Press, Seattle 1978.

Rainer C. Baum, 'Holocaust: Moral Indifference as *the* Form of Modern Evil', in Rosenberg and Myers (q.v.).

Zygmunt Bauman, *Modernity and the Holocaust*, Polity Press, Cambridge 1991.

Louis Begley, *Wartime Lies*, Pan Books, London 1992.

Saul Bellow, *Mr. Sammler's Planet*, Penguin, London 1972.

Bruno Bettelheim, 'Individual and Mass Behaviour in Extreme Situations', in E. E. Maccoby et al., eds., *Readings in Social Psychology*, Henry Holt, New York 1961.

Bruno Bettelheim, *The Informed Heart*, Penguin, London 1991.

Halina Birenbaum, *Hope is the Last to Die*, Twayne Publishers, New York 1971.

Gay Block and Malka Drucker, *Rescuers: Portraits of Moral Courage in the Holocaust*, Holmes & Meier, New York 1992.

Poul Borchsenius, 'Aspects of the Rescue of Danish Jews', *Wiener Library Bulletin* 22/4, New Series 13 (Autumn 1968).

Tadeusz Borowski, *This Way for the Gas, Ladies and Gentlemen*, Penguin, London 1976.

Marlon Brando (with Robert Lindsey), *Brando: Songs My Mother Taught Me*, Arrow, London 1995.

Stephen Eric Bronner, ed., *The Letters of Rosa Luxemburg*, Westview Press, Boulder 1978.

Christopher R. Browning, *Ordinary Men: Reserve Police Battalion 101 and the Final Solution in Poland*, HarperCollins, New York 1993.

Ferdinando Camon, *Conversations with Primo Levi*, The Marlboro Press, Marlboro (Vermont) 1989.

Arthur A. Cohen, *The Tremendum: A Theological Interpretation of the Holocaust*, Continuum, New York 1993.

Dan Cohn-Sherbok, *Holocaust Theology*, Lamp Press, London 1989.

Charlotte Delbo, *Auschwitz and After*, Yale University Press, New Haven and London 1995.

Terrence Des Pres, *The Survivor: An Anatomy of Life in the Death Camps*, Oxford University Press, New York 1976.

Isaac Deutscher, 'The Jewish Tragedy and the Historian', in his *The Non-Jewish Jew and other essays*, Oxford University Press, London 1968.

Fyodor Dostoyevsky, *The Brothers Karamazov*, Penguin, London 1993.

Deborah Dwork, *Children With A Star: Jewish Youth in Nazi Europe*, Yale University Press, New Haven 1991.

Ida Fink, *A Scrap of Time and other stories*, Peter Owen, London 1988.

Viktor E. Frankl, *Man's Search for Meaning*, Hodder & Stoughton, London 1987.

Henry Friedlander and Sybil Milton, eds., *The Holocaust:*

Ideology, Bureaucracy, and Genocide, Kraus International, New York 1980.

Henry Friedlander, 'Postscript: Toward a Methodology of Teaching about the Holocaust', in Friedlander and Milton (q.v.).

Saul Friedlander/Martin Broszat, 'A Controversy about the Historicization of National Socialism', *Yad Vashem Studies* 19 (1988).

Saul Friedlander, 'The "Final Solution": On the Unease in Historical Interpretation', in Peter Hayes, ed., *Lessons and Legacies: The Meaning of the Holocaust in a Changing World*, Northwestern University Press, Evanston 1991; reprinted in the item immediately following.

Saul Friedlander, *Memory, History, and the Extermination of the Jews of Europe*, Indiana University Press, Bloomington 1993.

Norman Geras, *The Legacy of Rosa Luxemburg*, Verso, London 1976.

Norman Geras, 'Literature of Revolution', *New Left Review* 113–114 (January/April 1979); reprinted in Norman Geras, *Literature of Revolution*, Verso, London 1986.

Norman Geras, *Marx and Human Nature: Refutation of a Legend*, Verso, London 1983.

Norman Geras, *Solidarity in the Conversation of Humankind: The Ungroundable Liberalism of Richard Rorty*, Verso, London 1995.

Ernest Germain [Ernest Mandel], 'A Biographical Sketch of Abram Leon', in Abram Leon, *The Jewish Question: A Marxist Interpretation*, Pathfinder Press, New York 1970.

Ernest Germain [Ernest Mandel], 'La question juive au lendemain de la deuxième guerre mondiale', afterword to Abram Léon, *Conception matérialiste de la question juive*, Éditions 'Pionniers', Paris 1946.

Martin Gilbert, *The Holocaust: The Jewish Tragedy*, Fontana, London 1987.

Eugene Heimler, *Night of the Mist*, Ace Books, London 1961.

Frances Henry, *Victims and Neighbours*, Bergin & Garvey, South Hadley (Mass.) 1984.

Etty Hillesum, *Etty: A Diary 1941–43*, Triad Grafton, London 1985.

Harold Hillman, 'The "Masters" of Torture', *AIBS Journal* (October/November 1992).

Eric Hobsbawm, 'Barbarism: A User's Guide', *New Left Review* 206 (July/August 1994).

Gordon J. Horwitz, *In the Shadow of Death: Living Outside the Gates of Mauthausen*, I. B. Tauris, London 1991.

Livia E. Bitton Jackson, *Elli: Coming of Age in the Holocaust*, Grafton, London 1984.

Karl Jaspers, *The Question of German Guilt*, Dial Press, New York 1947.

Hans Jonas, 'The Concept of God After Auschwitz: A Jewish Voice', in Rosenberg and Myers (q.v.); reprinted from *Journal of Religion* 67 (1987).

Immanuel Kant, *Foundations of the Metaphysics of Morals*, Bobbs-Merrill, Indianapolis and New York 1959.

Immanuel Kant, 'Perpetual Peace: A Philosophical Sketch', in Hans Reiss, ed., *Kant: Political Writings*, Cambridge University Press, Cambridge 1991.

Jacob Katz, 'Was the Holocaust Predictable?', in Y. Bauer and N. Rotenstreich, eds., *The Holocaust as Historical Experience*, Holmes & Meier, New York 1981.

Herbert Kelman, 'Violence without Moral Restraint', *Journal of Social Issues* 29/4 (1973).

Ian Kershaw, *Popular Opinion and Political Dissent in the Third Reich*, Clarendon Press, Oxford 1983.

Ernst Klee, Willi Dressen and Volker Riess, eds., *'Those were the Days': The Holocaust through the Eyes of the Perpetrators and Bystanders*, Hamish Hamilton, London 1991.

J. Knowlton and T. Cates (translators), *Forever in the Shadow of Hitler?*, Humanities Press, Atlantic Highlands 1993.

George M. Kren, 'The Holocaust as History', in Rosenberg and Myers (q.v.).

Ronnie S. Landau, *The Nazi Holocaust*, I. B. Tauris, London 1992.

Berel Lang, ed., *Writing and the Holocaust*, Holmes & Meier, New York 1988.

Lawrence L. Langer, 'The Dilemma of Choice in the Death-camps', in Roth and Berenbaum (q.v.); also in Rosenberg and Myers (q.v.).

Lawrence L. Langer, *Holocaust Testimonies: The Ruins of Memory*, Yale University Press, New Haven 1991.

Lawrence L. Langer, 'The Writer and the Holocaust Experience', in Friedlander and Milton (q.v.).

Claude Lanzmann, *Shoah: An Oral History of the Holocaust*, Pantheon, New York 1985.

Walter Laqueur, *The Terrible Secret*, Weidenfeld, London 1980.

Isabella Leitner, *Fragments of Isabella*, Thomas Y. Crowell, New York 1978.

Michael Lessnoff, *Social Contract*, Macmillan, London 1986.

Primo Levi, *Collected Poems*, Faber, London 1988.

Primo Levi, *The Drowned and the Saved*, Abacus, London 1989.

Primo Levi, *If This is a Man and The Truce*, Abacus, London 1987.

Primo Levi, *Moments of Reprieve*, Michael Joseph, London 1986.

Hanna Lévy-Hass, *Inside Belsen*, Harvester, Brighton 1982.

Abraham Lewin, *A Cup of Tears: A Diary of the Warsaw Ghetto*, Blackwell, Oxford 1988.

Ernest Mandel, Introduction to Leon Trotsky, *The Struggle Against Fascism in Germany* (q.v.).

Ernest Mandel, *The Meaning of the Second World War*, Verso, London 1986.

Ernest Mandel, 'Der Mensch ist das Hochste Wesen für den Menschen', in F. J. Raddatz, ed., *Warum Ich Marxist Bin*, Fischer, Frankfurt 1980.

Ernest Mandel, 'Prémisses matérielles, sociales et idéologiques du génocide nazi', in Y. Thanassekos and H. Wismann, eds., *Révision de l'histoire*, Cerf, Paris 1990.

Ernest Mandel, *Trotsky: A Study in the Dynamic of his Thought*, Verso, London 1979.

Ernest Mandel, *Trotsky As Alternative*, Verso, London 1995.

Ernest Mandel, 'Zum Historikerstreit', appendix to his *Der Zweite Weltkrieg*, ISP-Verlag, Frankfurt 1991.

Ernest Mandel – see also entries for Ernest Germain.

Michael Marrus, *The Holocaust in History*, Penguin, London 1987.

Micheline Maurel, *Ravensbrück*, Digit, London 1958.

Arno Mayer, *Why Did the Heavens Not Darken?*, Verso, London 1990.

Ralph Miliband, 'The Plausibility of Socialism', *New Left Review* 206 (July/August 1994).

Ralph Miliband, *Socialism for a Sceptical Age*, Polity, Cambridge 1994.

Barrington Moore Jr, *Reflections on the Causes of Human Misery*, Allen Lane, London 1972.

Odd Nansen, *From Day to Day*, Putnam, New York 1949.

Ernst Nolte, 'Between Historical Myth and Revisionism?', *Yad Vashem Studies* 19 (1988); also in Knowlton and Cates (q.v.).

Ernst Nolte, 'A Past That Will Not Pass Away', *Yad Vashem Studies* 19 (1988); also in Knowlton and Cates (q.v.).

Robert Nozick, *The Examined Life*, Simon & Schuster, New York 1989.

Angela Partington, ed., *The Oxford Dictionary of Quotations*, Oxford University Press, Oxford 1992.

Anna Pawelczynska, *Values and Violence in Auschwitz: A Sociological Analysis*, University of California Press, Berkeley 1979.

Patrick Riley, 'social contract', in David Miller, ed., *The Blackwell Encyclopaedia of Political Thought*, Blackwell, Oxford 1987.

Richard Rorty, *Contingency, Irony, and Solidarity*, Cambridge University Press, Cambridge 1989.

Richard Rorty, 'Human Rights, Rationality, and Sentimentality', in Stephen Shute and Susan Hurley, eds., *On Human Rights: The Oxford Amnesty Lectures 1993*, Basic Books, New York 1993.

Richard Rorty, 'Love and Money', *Common Knowledge* 1/1 (1992).

Alan Rosenberg and Gerald E. Myers, eds., *Echoes from the Holocaust: Philosophical Reflections on a Dark Time*, Temple University Press, Philadelphia 1988.

John K. Roth and Michael Berenbaum, eds., *Holocaust: Religious and Philosophical Implications*, Paragon House, New York 1989.

David Rousset, *The Other Kingdom*, Reynal & Hitchcock, New York 1947.

Richard L. Rubenstein, *After Auschwitz: Radical Theology and Contemporary Judaism*, Bobbs-Merrill, Indianapolis 1966.

Richard L. Rubenstein, *The Cunning of History: The Holocaust and the American Future*, Harper, New York 1987.

Richard L. Rubenstein, 'Some Perspectives on Religious Faith after Auschwitz', in Roth and Berenbaum (q.v.).

John Sabini and Maury Silver, 'On Destroying the Innocent with a Clear Conscience', in Joel Dimsdale, ed., *Survivors, Victims, and Perpetrators*, Hemisphere, Washington 1980; reprinted in their *Moralities of Everyday Life*, Oxford University Press, Oxford 1982.

Hilda Schiff, ed., *Holocaust Poetry*, HarperCollins, London 1995.

Gitta Sereny, *Into That Darkness*, André Deutsch, London 1991.

André Stein, *Quiet Heroes: True Stories of the Rescue of Jews by Christians in Nazi-occupied Holland*, Lester & Orpen Dennys, Toronto 1988.

George Steiner, 'The Long Life of Metaphor: An Approach to the "Shoah"', in Lang (q.v.); reprinted from *Encounter* 68 (February 1987).

Adina Blady Szwajger, *I Remember Nothing More*, Simon & Schuster, New York 1990.

Nechama Tec, *When Light Pierced the Darkness: Christian Rescue of Jews in Nazi-Occupied Poland*, Oxford University Press, Oxford 1986.

Laurence M. Thomas, 'Liberalism and the Holocaust', in Rosenberg and Myers (q.v.).

Laurence M. Thomas, *Vessels of Evil: American Slavery and the Holocaust*, Temple University Press, Philadelphia 1993.

Tzvetan Todorov, *Facing the Extreme: Moral Life in the Concentration Camps*, Metropolitan Books, New York 1996.

Enzo Traverso, *Les Marxistes et la question juive*, La Brèche, Montreuil 1990.

Enzo Traverso, 'Trotsky et la question juive', *Quatrième Internationale* 36 (1990).

Leon Trotsky, *1905*, Allen Lane, London 1972.

Leon Trotsky, *On the Jewish Question*, Pathfinder Press, New York 1970.

Leon Trotsky, *The Struggle Against Fascism in Germany*, Pathfinder Press, New York 1971.

Jiri Weil, *Life with a Star*, Fontana, London 1990.

Elie Wiesel, *One Generation After*, Random House, New York 1970.

Elie Wiesel, 'Talking and Writing and Keeping Silent', in Roth and Berenbaum (q.v.).

Elie Wiesel, *The Town Beyond the Wall*, Schocken, New York 1982.

Binjamin Wilkomirski, *Fragments: Memories of a Childhood, 1939–1948*, Picador, London 1996.

Leni Yahil, 'Jews in Concentration Camps in Germany Prior to World War II', in Y. Gutman and A. Saf, eds., *The Nazi Concentration Camps*, Yad Vashem, Jerusalem 1984.

Henri Zukier, 'The Twisted Road to Genocide: On the Psychological Development of Evil During the Holocaust', *Social Research* 61 (1994).

Index